CHICAGO TAXI CONFESSIONS

By

Paul Oranika

This book is a work of non-fiction. Names and places have been changed to protect the privacy of all individuals. The events and situations are true.

ISBN: 1-4033-7646-8 (e-book)
ISBN: 1-4033-7647-6 (Paperback)

Library of Congress Control Number: 2002095282

This book is printed on acid free paper.

Printed in the United States of America
Bloomington, IN

1st Books - rev. 11/13/02

Dedication

To My Mother

Mrs. Helen Nwaka Oranika

Acknowledgements

This book would not have been possible without the support of all the members of my family. From my wife Nkiru, to my four children, who endured long periods of time without me. Special thanks go to my daughters Amaka, and Nkem, and son IB for proofreading my initial manuscript. Apologies to my son Paul Jr. for all the missed time for basketball, partly due to the project. Special thanks as well to my sister Vicky, for her help and support. I would like to thank all my friends for their moral support for this project. Ms. Alexander provided me with some of the photographs for this book, a special thanks to her. To some of my friends who actually told me that writing and publishing is reserved for celebrities and published authors, may I say thank you as well, however wrong they may be. It is incongruous to complete this segment without extending a warm and sincere gratitude to all my passengers, who provided me with some of their humor stories, bravo to them all. Last but not the least, a special thanks to the rest of my passengers, who encouraged me to write this book. In fact, their encouragement ranks high in motivating me and hence this work.

Table Of Contents

Section III
Taxi Humor Stories

Section IV
Driver/Passenger Relations

Introduction

Over the years, many of my numerous passengers asked me, to tell them stories about unusual things that happened in my taxi. Others would ask for my funny experiences and humor stories. Very often I do tell them these stories. My passengers loved these stories very much. Some would suggest to me to do a book based on these stories, because there are a lot of people who would like to read such a book. The success of the popular Hbo program "Taxi Confessions" was often drawn to my attention.

Soon I began to contemplate if I should undertake such a project. Many people are intimidated by writing, myself included, but these suggestions were actually increasing by the day, and it became apparent to me that people are generally obsessed with taxi, and funny stories. But can a Chicago cab driver complete such an intimidating process of writing a book? I mentioned the idea to another cab driver friend of mine, who discouraged me, by reminding me of the huddles involved in writing and publishing. Unless one is a published author, celebrity or a politician, the road to writing and publishing is an obstacle course, some of my friends warned me. At the same time, my passengers continued to encourage me that I could pull off such a project.

Initially I took these suggestions as flattery, but then I started to note that my tips from the passengers I told these stories were usually more than the normal tips I get. On longer trips, which sometimes take over an hour, I told longer stories. Generally people use their time inside the taxi to catch up with all their voice mail messages, or to make their phone calls. I had to find a way to survey my passengers about the prospects of such a book, without disturbing their peace in the taxi.

A thought came to my mind one day. I put up a sign inside my taxi, its contents read, "Short taxi stories available for your entertainment", it was a way for me to actually see if there was an appetite for such stories. I was not prepared for what followed. During the small time that this sign was up, I was getting in some cases thirty to fifty percent tips from the passengers I told these stories. It dawned on me that the market was out there for such books.

There was a particular trip from O'Hare International airport, to Oak Park, Illinois a suburb of Chicago. A young lady asked me to tell her some taxi humor stories or unusual things that happened in my taxi. I started telling her the story of my homosexual passenger, a story you will subsequently read in the chapters to come. The point here however, is that the trip was about to end, and my passenger was determined, that she must hear the story in its entirety. She asked me, to pull over about one block to her house, and tell her the rest of the story. She also asked me to leave the meter running. My goodness, I said to myself, so this story had that much value, I wondered.

From that point onwards, I seriously started considering writing a book based on these stories. This book was therefore motivated in part by all of my passengers, who encouraged me to write about the events in my taxi, and other humor stories, an effort that culminated in this work.

This is also an effort for me, to prove to myself that those years of college and graduate school were not wasted, with a redundant job that needed no advanced skills. But don't get me wrong; taxi work requires a lot of talent and concentration. It involves a high degree of alertness, but any one with such qualities could be a taxi driver. Think of the taxi driver as your airline pilot. They have some things in common. When you hire your taxi driver, you are in essence trusting your life to his care during the ride, the same way you trust your life to an airline pilot during your flight. I know people don't generally make this analogy, but it is a fact of life.

Another factor that also motivated this book indirectly was an argument, which I had with another taxi driver. I was in the number one spot on the taxi stand, meaning that I should pick up the next arriving passenger out of the North Western train station.

This is a busy downtown train station on Madison Avenue. Another cab driver had just dropped his passenger in front of the taxi line, and for some reason wanted to cheat, by picking up another fare without taking his turn on the queue.

I told him that he could not do that, because he was not in the number one loading position.

Meanwhile a passenger had already entered his taxi, but on hearing the argument, this passenger decided to leave his taxi for mine. This driver was mad and he started, cursing me. I remember him saying that taxi drivers are so mean to one another. I recalled to him that I waited through the line for my turn, while he did not. He added that Taxi drivers are bunch of uneducated and unmannered group of people adding that he could work in another occupation because he was educated, while I could not because I was not.

So this is an effort to prove to myself that I could do something other than driving a taxi. If this book is successful, and I have a feeling that it may be, then a new writer is born. The Chicago cab driver is fairly an educated class in themselves, although I must add that the taxi culture is inherently competitive. The occupation is extremely stressful, as you would read in the chapters to come.

Taxi culture is inherently contradictory with civilized behavior.

I have heard people say that cabdrivers, have no courtesy, they cut you off your lanes, and hardly yield to other drivers. While my purpose here is not to defend taxi drivers' driving habits, I am attempting to explain reasons why they do things their way.

Majority of the cab drivers in Chicago, and possibly in most other major cities in this Country are recent emigrants. Driving in third world countries is like survival of the fittest. With that experience in their background, coupled with the stresses of dealing with traffic congestion in the cities, plus passenger pressures, you create a super stressed and aggressive individual.

A taxi driver must hustle for fares. Taxi culture and passenger behavior warrants that.

When I first started as a new cab driver, I was a "gentle cab driver", in the sense that I often yielded to other cab drivers. But this often meant that I missed the passenger standing ahead. A passenger may flag me down, but soon they jump into another cab that dives across two or three lanes of traffic to get to them first. Sooner or later I started to learn the competitive lessons. Such competition, as rude as they may be, often translates into cash in the driver's pocket.

My first day was a little intimidating, because, obtaining the chauffer license is one thing but soon I was faced with the real situation of trying to figure out addresses and destinations some obvious and others are not. But as a city chauffer license holder, I had to prove to the passengers that I am the expert, safe, and well trained professional which the city certified me to be.

Sometimes it worked, but in some cases I had to swallow my pride and ask my passenger for some help. Most passengers would gladly help, but every now and then I run into a situation where the passenger is hostile. My experience for the first day was quite interesting, as well as intriguing.

I was amazed at the intimate level of passenger conversations inside the taxi. Such talks only belonged in the bedroom, I thought, but such conversations soon became an interesting aspect of the job.

Many of such conversations are still vivid in my memory.

Many of my trips are short and sometimes the trips end before the main points of the conversations are made, but there are also longer trips that take up to one and half hours to complete. Some of the wildest stories I have heard were usually told on Saturday and Friday nights, and I am pretty sure you already know the reasons why.

Those evenings are usually party time for the crowd in Chicago, and I must reassure you that it is a serious business in Chicago land. Some bars in the city have extended hours, enabling them to open up to five o'clock in the morning on Saturday nights.

Chicago is blessed with many young professionals. Many of them live in Lincoln Park. These young professionals are fairly liberal in their views, and pursuit of happiness seems to be their, modus operandi. They have money to spend as well. To many cab drivers in Chicago, Fridays and Saturdays represent their paydays. Sometimes it is possible for a cabbie to make up to fifty percent of their weekly intake on those two days. Thousands of other suburban young adults also pour into the downtown areas, roaming the streets. They hop from one bar to another, jumping in and out of taxis all night long. Chicago cabbies love such nights.

This book is divided into four sections. The first section includes a personal account of my experiences as a Chicago cab driver. Included in this section are stories based on taxi operating environment in Chicago, as well as the inherent dangers associated with the occupation. The second section focuses on taxi stories and in-taxi conversations. Some of the stories in this section came from my passengers.

The third section contains brief humor stories from both myself, and my passengers.

The fourth section concludes with suggestions to help you make your cab driver happy.

Some of my most favorite short cuts are provided as a concluding chapter. It's a must read for those of you who drive in Chicago, alternative short cuts would prove valuable indeed in avoiding some of the traffic bottlenecks in the city.

This book would satisfy your laughter needs for a long time to come. The best way to enjoy the stories is by reading few chapters at a time. You may continue reading to the last chapter if you want, either way, you would get your money's worth.

Section I
Chicago Taxi Environment

Chapter 1
Who Wants To Be A Chicago Cab Driver

Anyone aspiring to drive taxi in Chicago or for that matter anywhere, must leave their ego at home, before getting on the wheels of their taxi. This is a warning that comes from years of experience. The taxi driver is insulted and ridiculed in many more ways than you can imagine. I remember when the Clinton scandal was at its peak, one afternoon there was a guest who was commenting on the popular NPR program, "All Things Considered".

The topic that day was how the Clinton scandal has helped to educate the general population about the American Judicial process. I do not quarrel with that characterization, but my problem was the statement made by a guest on the program. He said "Even cab drivers can now lecture you on the meaning of high crimes and misdemeanors" Give me a break please, is the speaker implying that cab drivers don't understand English, nor own radios or television, or in a nut shell-a bunch of illiterates.

I would allow you a few seconds to get your laughter out of the way, but it does help to make my point that society assigns a very little value or for that matter respect to the taxi occupation. To the commentator, let me remind him that some Chicago taxi drivers are college and university graduates, some of the drivers hold advanced degrees,

As I stated earlier, they come from every corner of the world, and many of them are qualified enough to give lessons on "high crimes and misdemeanors", even before the manifestation of the "Clinton Scandal". People are drawn to taxi work because of the relative freedom and flexibility that it offers, an opportunity that many immigrants and students find suitable. Many of the stories you will read in this book would help you to understand how society stereotypes the taxi occupation, and hence taxi drivers.

Chapter 2
Coping With The Job

One of the first lessons that a new taxi driver should learn is that majority of the passengers using taxi service in Chicago have little or no respect for the driver. I try to avoid generalities, and that's why I used the word "majority". There are some passengers that truly understand, and respect cab drivers. But having said that, I must quickly add that such riders are in the minority.

Taxi work does not appeal to many individuals for many reasons. It is a very dangerous occupation. In fact it has been said many times that taxi work is the most dangerous occupation in America. The National Institute for Occupational Safety said that taxi driving is the most dangerous job in the United States, and the nearest runner-up is Law enforcement. Why is this so you may ask, well the answer is simple. A taxi driver is simply a sitting duck. Despite the fact that a cab driver picks up any member of the society, both the good and the bad, taking them to remote and dangerous locations, they have little chances of defending themselves against a sudden attack.

But before I look into the dangers of robbery and being killed in the process, let me discuss other dangers inherent in the taxi occupation, for instance the stress related challenges of driving in big cities such as New York, Los Angeles or Chicago, could not be underestimated. Traffic related stress could really get to you in Chicago. No wonder we hear of road rage these days, this is simply the demonstration of such traffic stress, which gets to a point that drivers overreact to little traffic altercations, like a lane change. For a cab driver he has to deal with such situation during the entire shift which usually last anywhere from twelve to fifteen hours a day, the magnitude of this problem is often understated.

People generally ask me how many hours do I work a day, and they are surprised when I respond with twelve hours or more. The way taxi business is structured is such that a typical cab driver in Chicago may spend up to eight hours before they make enough money to cover their daily overhead. A typical daily cost to lease a cab, for twelve-hours in Chicago is about seventy dollars. When you add your expense for the ever-skyrocketing gas, which may cost an average driver about thirty dollars a day, your daily expense averages about one hundred and ten dollars.

So an average driver puts in twelve hours dealing with the bone crushing traffic situation. Driving a taxi in Chicago means that the driver must watch out for the CTA busses whose drivers always remind other road users that they own the streets of the windy city. When they change lanes, they often issue no signals, and drivers in the lanes the busses are trying to enter have little choice but to run for their dear life, the simple reason being that the busses are much bigger than other vehicles.

Cab drivers also worry about pedestrians, who have simply relinquished their road safety responsibilities to the drivers, some cross the streets when they should be waiting for the signals. But Chicago cab drivers have better manners than cab drivers in the Big Apple {New York City} at least they wait for pedestrians to cross the streets even when the signals forbid them from doing so. I do not imply here that New York cabbies would run you over, if you stand on their way, but please don't take a chance like that.

Cab drivers are also on the look out for other cabs, I must admit that other taxis actually constitute a bigger problem for drivers than the CTA busses. Chicago cabs are hustlers, they fight for fares, and some may dive across three lanes of traffic to catch a waiting fare.

But part of their aggressive behavior comes from the competitive nature of their job, in addition to the fact that, they spend long hours on the streets of Chicago. They have become masters of the streets and corners of the windy city, as cabbies reason.

Chapter 3
Getting Around Chicago

The first quick lesson I learnt on my first day was that many Chicago passengers would tell you the name of the building they want, but not the address. My first passenger was picked up at Michigan avenue and Roosevelt intersection. She requested that I take her to Leo Burnett building. I did not recognize the building by its' name but I was pretty confident that I could find it, if only she told me the building's address.

I turned the meter on, and started driving north on Michigan Avenue. I thought about asking her for some directions but I saw the look on her face and my instinct told me that this is not a friendly passenger. Well I continued heading north but obviously driving too slow for the car behind me, whose driver flashed its high beam lights, signifying me to move faster,or get out of her way. I decided to choose the later, and I signaled to the right, attempting to enter the right lane.

The Chicago Transit Authority bus on the right lane quickly accelerated, an indication he was not going to let me in, meanwhile I was approaching Randolph street. I then decided to ask her for an address because I was getting frustrated with the way things were going.If that meant swallowing my ego, so be it.

I politely asked her for an address since I did not recognize the building by its name, as I slowed down, across two lanes of traffic, into the right lane. I confronted for a second time a wall of CTA busses that stretched the entire block. There was no place.for me to go, as the busses indicated by their action that I do not belong in those lanes.

Taxi cabs and CTA busses struggle for lanes on Michigan Avenue

I continued to drive slowly on the center lane as I waited for my passenger to give me an address. Few cars that managed to overtake my cab gave me a finger as they passed me. Who cares about fingers anymore, after all in the course of a day's work, a Chicago cab driver may get twenty fingers. A stoplight ahead turned red as I approached the intersection, a welcome relief sign for me at that point.

My passenger suddenly asked me, "Where are you from"? She said. I pretended as if I did not hear her question, despite her loud voice. I asked again for an address and this time she told me, that she was not sure of the address, adding that she would point out the building as soon as I get close to it.

Soon I approached Wacker drive and confronted another mini crisis- there was a no left turn signal conspicuously displayed at the intersection of Wacker and Michigan avenue. I made a quick decision to turn right into Wacker drive and an immediate U-turn into westbound Wacker drive, and it worked. I was lucky though because the U-turn was illegal, but there was no cop around. All the time my passenger was quiet watching the situation play itself out.

As soon as I completed the U-turn, I continued heading westward on Wacker drive. When I crossed State Street, she pointed to a skyscraper on the left side of the street and asked me to pull over. The fare was five dollars and eighty cents, and she gave me six dollars. I reached for a twenty cent change, thinking she would ask me to keep that, but I was wrong. She collected her twenty cent change from me and exited the taxi with a bang, noting that I should learn the streets of Chicago before driving a taxi. Meanwhile I took note of the address on the building which was 35 West Wacker drive an address I would never again forget.

After this ordeal, I decided to go for a coffee brake, so I went to Mike's restaurant, a popular place for cab drivers in Chicago. I walked into the restaurant, and asked another cab driver, if I could join him at his table, and he reluctantly said fine. You know for some reason, cab drivers often recognize other cab drivers, don't ask why because I don't know the answer to that question. My guess is that their instinct correctly guides their thinking at that time. When I walked into the restaurant, out of over twenty-five people seated at different tables, I walked straight to this guy.

I introduced myself to him, as we waited for coffee. I decided to tell him what happened on my first trip of my taxi-driving career, obviously seeking for an advice from him. I was not sure what his reaction would be like, for one thing, this guy looked unfriendly. So I told him in detail about the trip that I just had, expecting to get a friendly reaction, but Peter as he introduced himself was even more merciless as was my first passenger, telling me that if I did not know Leo Burnett building, that I had no business driving taxi in Chicago.

I explained to Peter that I scored eighty five percent, in the taxi exams. He was not impressed. He reaches for a cigarette, and started smoking. I thought about leaving his table at that point, because the smoke was bothering me, but he was seating on the smoking side, so I decided to manage up with him. Soon the waitress served us coffee. Peter told me that passing the taxi test was one thing, but the score was quite meaningless if I could not identify a land mark- Leo Burnett building. For a moment, I thought whether this job was really something that I should be doing because of the two experiences I had so far. Peter told me that he has driven taxi in Chicago for 25 years, basically since he emigrated from Greece. "How in the world were you able to keep your body and soul together all those years"? I asked, "Who told you that my body is still together" Peter said. "I do not have much feelings on my left leg" he told me. His doctor warned him that he does not have enough exercise, and that blood flow to his lower body is impaired by his long sitting position in the cab. Why can't you quit the job? I asked Peter. "I have many dependants," Peter said. "What about you"?

Peter asked me. Well this is my first day of driving, I am not sure if I would be doing this job next year I told him.

At the end of the conversation, Peter told me, that I should ask passengers for route suggestions if I was not sure, he said that most of the Chicago passengers would be more than glad to give me directions because they think they know the city more than the average cab driver.

Peter however gave me a good suggestion that I should buy a small book that was compiled for new cab drivers. Such a book would prove very useful to me, he said. I quickly purchased the book from the restaurant and indeed it was helpful, particularly in suburban destinations and highway system in the greater Chicago land.

With some renewed confidence, I was now prepared for the next fare and I decided to check out the Union Station Terminal.

The Union Station is a busy spot to solicit for passengers. I decided to check it up because one of my friends told me, that sometimes one could pick up long fares going to the suburbs. The line was fairly long, but I waited in line anyway. About twenty minutes later, a Hispanic passenger walked out of the train station and entered my taxi. This time, the problem that surfaced was a situation that I had no control of. My passenger speaks only Spanish, and I only speak English. When you are faced with such a situation, there was basically no room for compromise. His questions along with the hand sign language accompanying them, were met with my answers in English.

I was able to pick up a few words he consistently mentioned, which became the clue to his destination. His emphasis on the word "Lagoon" led me to believe he was referring to Lake Michigan, because he simultaneously pointed in the direction of the lake, so based on that alone I took the fare hoping to figure out the rest as we continued on the trip. As soon as I exited from the station I quickly turned into Jackson Ave, a one-way street heading towards lake Michigan. Meanwhile my passenger confirmed that we were heading in the right direction by nodding his head.

When we reached the end of Jackson Street, he directed me to make a left turn into Lakeshore drive, a coastal highway running alongside lake Michigan. As soon as we made the turn we were heading north on Lakeshore drive. Eventually we exited into

Cars rolling along on Chicago's Lakeshore Drive

Montrose Avenue at his request and ended up at the 4400 block of N.Sheridan road, where the fare terminated.

I was not aware that he had no money with him to pay for the fare; my passenger was counting on getting the money from his girl friend, who lives there.

He made a cell phone call to her as soon as we arrived in the compound.

I consistently pointed to the fare, drawing his attention to that, expecting money so I can move on. He sat quietly at the back, but soon his girl friend emerged from the building.

She said to me "Gracias amigo". I was able to put that one together, because if you live in Chicago, there is no way you could not understand what it meant.

"Gracias" meant "thank you", while "Amigo" meant "Friend". Welcome to Spanish 101, I repeated "Gracias Amiga", because she is a woman. She looked at the meter and the fare was eleven dollars and some change. She gave me twelve dollars, as I reached for the change, she told me to keep it. My passenger walked out of the taxi, he smiled, and waved goodbye, as I pulled out of the building.

Chapter 4
Meeting Your Chicago Cab Driver

Chicago cab drivers come from basically every corner of the world. The majority of them have Arabic heritage, with Pakistanis outnumbering the others. Nigerians and Ghanaians represent the majority of those from the African continent.

There are small but increasing numbers of both Latinos and White emigrants from Eastern Europe and Countries of the former Soviet Union. African Americans are the majority among the native born Americans who drive taxi in the city. White Americans traditionally are not drawn to taxi work as an occupation although, they own most of the medallions for taxi business in the city, but a limited number of them drive as well.

It is therefore correct to say that an overwhelming majority of Chicago cab drivers are recent immigrants, most of them migrated from Countries with political and economic instabilities. Taxi drivers in Chicago do not have any strong union as a result of the international make-up of the drivers.

Many of the cab patrons in Chicago simply feel that Chicago taxi drivers do not understand the city, as a result there are pressures on the Consumer Services Department of the City of Chicago to enact tougher standards for persons aspiring to drive taxi in the city.

The dilemma facing city officials is the reality that taxi work does not appeal to most Americans, if emigrants are eliminated from taxi work, literally there would be no taxis on the streets. A recent one day strike in the city had a devastating effect on businesses and companies whose customers, and employees rely on taxis as a way of getting to their jobs.

Well over fifteen thousand individuals hold the city of Chicago Chauffer licenses. This figure includes Limo Drivers as well, but majority of those licenses are issued to cab drivers. Many of the cab drivers work on part time basis.

Taxi driving in Chicago, begins with the completion of a 5-day course about the city and its environment, interesting places, highways and streets. Upon completion of the course, a written examination is administered. An applicant must score eighty percent or better to pass the test. A police crime check is then undertaken, and if everything checks out well, then the individual is issued a city Chauffer license.

Where Do Chicago Cab Drivers Live?

Majority of the Chicago cabbies live outside the loop, for obvious reasons-rent in the loop is beyond their income. An average two-bedroom condo in the loop costs about $300,000. Another factor why Chicago cabbies live outside the loop is the segregated housing pattern in Chicago. One of my tourist passengers once asked me, why there are no racial conflicts in Chicago as in New York City. Well I told him the answer is simple-the races live apart in various ethnic neighborhoods. Basically every large ethnic group has its ethnic neighborhood in Chicago.

African Americans live largely on the Southside and parts of the Westside. Hispanics and Puerto Ricans live on the Westside. Chinese live in China Town. Indians and Pakistanis despite their countries' differences over Kashmir live together near Lawrence and Devon neighborhoods. Italians have Little Italy, while the Greeks occupy Greek town. The Poles and Germans all have ethnic neighborhoods of their own. Even new groups from the African continent are concentrating on the far north side. A small enclave of Nigerians is developing in the far North side and Calumet City. Whites live in Gold coast, Lincoln Park, and the suburbs.

When new emigrant cab drivers move to Chicago, they find out that distinct ethnic neighborhoods supportive of their culture and heritage are already in place, hence they move into such places. Chicago cab drivers are commuters as well; some may drive up to forty minutes to reach the loop.

Chapter 5
Driving In The Loop

Taxi work in the city operates in two –12 hour shifts. The first shift runs from 5am to 5pm, and the second shift from 5pm to 5am.Many of the cab drivers working in the loop prefer the 5am to 5pm shift; it is the time that offices and businesses in the loop are open. Many of the cabbies operating in the loop generally start between 5 and 6am, hoping to catch the morning rush hour, lasting from about 6am to 10am. The morning rush hour may generate about fifty or sixty dollars for the early birds.

By 11am most other cabbies have all arrived in the loop. This group consists of mostly owner- operators {those who lease on weekly basis and carrying out maintenance of their leased vehicles} and independent medallion owners. Competition is fierce among loop drivers. They clutter the streets of the loop, waiting for passengers like hawks diving to catch a prey.

By noontime latecomers including mostly older drivers have all made it to the loop. This is also the check out time for the hotel guests, and some cabbies would line up at the loop hotels hoping to pick up an airport fare. I belong to the early bird group, although I generally work longer hours as a routine. The hotel stand is simply a gamble. I have waited for as long as one hour, only to pick up a three to four dollar fare. Many drivers are pissed at such fares, because cabbies roaming the streets make an average of fifteen dollars an hour.

Competition among cab drivers is very stiff, as they fight for fares. They do not yield to one another. Cab drivers with Arabic heritage cooperate with one another compared to other groups. Once a friend of mine cut me off my lane to pick up a fare ahead, pretending that he did not see me. Once the passenger was safely seated in his cab, he now waved at me, telling me that he did not see me. I replied him, "Yeah right" signaling him to just move on.

If you don't want to be run over by a Chicago cab driver, your best bet is to stay clear of the distance between him and a luggage-carrying passenger. Cab drivers in Chicago reason that if you are carrying a luggage, you must be going to the airport.

There is also competition from the airport shuttles and the ever-present Limos. Some of the hotel doormen would arrange with some

Limo drivers for the airport fares. They get a little kickback for such services. The Hyatt Regency doormen are notorious for such practice.

Some lucky cabbies may indeed pick up airport fares from the loop locations. It is always a good feeling when such uncommon event happens. A typical airport fare is about $35 dollars. Occasionally I get $40 from generous tippers. The airport cabstand is a different ball game. It requires a different strategy of its own. Some cab drivers only work at the airport. Others would only stay at the airport if a fare takes them there. Other drivers simply would drop passengers and head back to the loop empty. My judgment of whether to stay or not, depends on the day and the circumstance. Waiting time at O'Hare and the traffic time back to the loop are some of the factors, which I consider.

Pandemonium In The Loop

Chicago cabbies have to deal with all the lost tourists drivers. While I admit that Chicago needs all their dollars, the city would be better off, if they left their cars behind. Many of the congestion in the city are caused by people who are lost on the streets, and simply have no clues where they are.

I would also include many of the suburban drivers in this category, but as a taxi driver, tourists make my driving experience somewhat easier, because they leave longer spaces between them and the cars they are following, making it easier for taxi drivers to change lanes much faster. The reason why they leave such long gaps is two fold; they are trying to figure out their next direction to turn; others are driving while exploring many sights in the city.

If you want to avoid tourists in Chicago, your strategy is to take alternative routes, for instance if you are going north from south Michigan avenue, avoid Michigan avenue, take Dearborn like many cab drivers, most often tourists know about Michigan avenue, but they fail to realize that there are many other streets that run northwards alongside Michigan avenue. My most favorite short cuts are provided in section IV of this book, for those who must drive in the windy city, it is a valuable information.

Traffic on Ohio and Ontario streets are usually heavy at all times, I refer to those streets as tourist allies, because they link up with the Interstate 90/94 which most tourists use to enter and exit from the city, forgetting that there are over ten other exits and entrance ramps into and out of Chicago.

Some of the biggest challenges facing taxi-drivers in Chicago include how to avoid the "Kamikaze " delivery cyclists, who as far as I am concerned are suicidal candidates. They would challenge you to run them down if you like. They cross red lights at forty miles an hour speed. How could anyone wishing to live, shoot across busy intersections at such speeds, not having a clear view of traffic coming from the other direction, this to me clearly defies logic and reason.

Traffic in Chicago is particularly bad and hectic during the summer months; in fact there is a joke that people make about that, by saying that there are two seasons in Chicago-Winter, and Construction seasons. With the closure of Lower Wacker drive, the year 2001 was a nightmare for traffic. Many Cabbies see the Lower Wacker system as a way of getting around the traffic in the loop. With the closure of the upper and lower Wacker drives, it created a nightmare, and for cab drivers, it created another headache.

These traffic challenges, make the work of the taxi driver very difficult. Cab drivers face the danger of being injured or killed on the job. But many Chicago passengers actually add more stress to the job, by pressuring cab drivers to get them to their destinations in as little time as possible. Some of those requests do not make sense because there is no way for the driver to get them to their locations in time if such passengers don't allow enough time for even traffic light delays.

Chapter 6
The Chicago Rush Hour

Rush hour in the windy city is simply chaos; in fact a better description would be “Stress hour” Basically every one leaving the offices is in a terrible hurry to get on the train. During the morning and evening rush hours, the trains run more frequently, so I always wonder what a ten to fifteen minutes delay in getting home would cost the commuters. For many commuters, the rush to get home often ends up in arguments with their spouses, for the simple reason that both parties are tense returning from work. Taxi-drivers often listen to passengers, requesting the driver to do what is otherwise impossible.

That reminds me of one of such request; I picked up a passenger at the Water Tower Mall about five o’clock in the evening, considered the height of evening rush hour in Chicago. She was going to the Union station about twenty blocks away. She rushed into the taxi and told me that she simply cannot miss the next train, because she must get home right away, I asked her how much time does she have, and she replied eight minutes. I did not want to waste any more time so I took off, but I knew, that it was impossible for her to make that train, for the simple reason that going through twenty blocks at rush hour, means, going through twenty traffic lights. Assuming that you catch twelve or more lights, and spending one to two minutes per light, simply means that from a mathematical point of view, there is no way one can make it to the Union station in eight minutes. I knew that, and honestly speaking, I believe my passenger knows that reality as well, but we are going to give it a try anyway.

Two minutes later I told her that there is no way for her to catch that train, because it usually takes fifteen minutes to get to the Union Station by that time of the day. As I approached the next light it turned red, and my passenger actually wanted me to beat the red light, but I explained to her that I don't go through red lights, and that I don't appreciate pressure, when I am driving. My best time to the Union Station was twelve minutes despite the fact that I really pushed it.

She missed the train quite all right, and there was no tip of cause for me, but I managed to keep my sanity together. Cab drivers somewhat contribute to the problem, by actually trying to catch trains that are un-cacheable. Their thinking is that the amount of tip they would receive, may be greater, if they increased their speed, or by attempting to go through the changing yellow/red lights.

That may be true in some cases, but my experience tells me, that it is not usually the case. But for me, I have done things that way, during the earlier years of my taxi-driving career, but over the years I asked myself, if an additional one dollar tip is worth both my life or my passenger's life. Nevertheless I try my best to help, only when my mind tells me that such a request is within reach.

Chapter 7
City Taxi Ordinances

City ordinance in Chicago makes it mandatory that cab drivers must not reject fares based on the destination; I understand the reasoning behind this law, because minorities find it hard to hale taxis in Chicago. Obviously there is a contradiction in enforcing this statute. Cab drivers are not employees of the city. Although the city has the right to regulate taxi business in the name of public safety, implementation of this particular statute presents a challenge to city regulators. While this law remains in the book, cab driver's instinct remains the guiding principle in the decisions, which the drivers make, about what passengers to pick up. Cab drivers are subjected to random drug tests, while I do not quarrel with this ordinance, I have problems with the way the law is implemented. There are no specific standards; sometimes it is administered at the discretion of the attending employee.

For instance, there was a day that I went to renew my chauffer license, and I mistakenly answered an attendant's question to me with "sir', instead of "madam". She thought that it was deliberate, and got upset over that. Before I could render an apology to her, she asked me, “Do you want to go for a drug test”? I said “no madam”, making sure this time that I did not use “sir” again, which would have automatically earned me a drug test.

Not to say that I was worried of a drug test, but many cab drivers worry about the cost of the test as well as the time it takes to complete such test. Traffic Aides often cite cab drives for offences by standing on the street corners, armed with a pen and a ticket. Many times cab drivers, and other motorists do not even know, what the tickets were written for. Flying tickets are forwarded to drivers through their registered addresses.

There are many other cab ordinances in Chicago that may not stand a legal challenge. Sometimes cab drivers are cited for dropping passengers. The problem is that you pick up a fare and when you get to the destination, your passenger orders you to stop. Often some passengers would tell you the exact spot to stop, within some inches or feet. The cab driver stops, and a police or traffic aide staff cites them for that.

Under such a situation the cab driver is victimized in the sense that you have a customer wanting to get out of the taxi, and city officials are saying that you could not drop them at that point, and there are no identified drop off points near that vicinity. The city administrators have not done all it could do, to help make the job of cab drivers easier and safer, than what it is now.

As a cab driver, I know a lot of the hot spots where all kinds of illegal activities are being conducted, it is one thing to ask cab drivers to go to those areas, but why doesn't the police, patrol such areas? You may find a lot of the cops in safer areas of the city; many in coffee parlors, or White Hen Pantries reading magazines. Sometimes there are two or three, controlling traffic at an intersection, standing and waiting to write flying tickets against cab drivers and other motorists.

Flying tickets generate a lot of revenue for the city; it boils down to money, after all a city cop and traffic aide writing flying tickets generate more revenues for the city. I would suggest that the mayor should create special patrol units for the hot spots in the city; it would create a better sense of security for everyone, cab drivers included.

Better still many of the traffic aides should be posted to patrol these troubled areas of the city, along with the police. My feeling is that such efforts would better serve the citizens of Chicago in the long run, by helping to keep the streets safe, and free of drug dealers.

Chapter 8
Trip To The Board Of Trade

I have learnt over the years, not to personalize things that passengers say to me, but rather take them as part of the experiences inherent with the occupation. Sometimes one is tempted to overreact, as human beings, but with more years of being on the wheels of a taxi, adjustment starts to set in. New drivers may find it particularly difficult to cope up with things that people say to them, but there are ways to diffuse such situations, through the use of humor.

I once picked up some traders, going to the board of trade on the corner of Jackson and LaSalle Streets in the Loop. They were four in number, three sat on the back seat and one passenger walked up to the front seat. As soon as he opened the front door of the taxi, he found an Investors Business Daily newspaper on the front seat.

He picked it up from the seat, and said to me "Oh! Somebody left their newspaper, in your taxi", "Can you do me a favor"? I asked him. He said, "What favor" I said "Can you please return the newspaper to him, since you know the owner" All the four passengers started laughing, at that point I knew it was a good joke, and I started laughing as well. I then told them that I bought that newspaper to track my investments, the conversation then shifted to the stock markets, soon it was time for them to drop out, still getting a thrill from my humor, they gave me a three dollar tip on top of the fare of four dollars, I generally get one dollar tip for such fares. The point here is that in my passenger's sub-conscious mind, something told him that a cab driver has no need for the business newspaper.

The newspaper therefore he theorized, was not mine. He decided that the newspaper belonged to the previous passenger who rode in the taxi. Chicago taxi drivers face some more serious problems apart from the stereotyping from passengers. The next series of chapters highlights these problems.

Chapter 9
Facing A Drawn Pistol

I had just dropped of a fare at Sheridan and Belmont area, and was heading back to the loop. There are two lanes of traffic on Sheridan road southbound; a patrol car was driving on the curbside lane, while I drove alongside him on the inner lane. On approaching Sheridan road and Wellington, my taxi and the squad car drove through the changing yellow light. The officer turned on his emergency lights.

I thought he just received an emergency call on his radio, and I slowed down for him, but the squad car slowed down as well. The officer signaled me to pull over. I did, and he parked behind me, he walked towards me, and asked me for my license. I passed it on to him.

I thought about asking him what was wrong, but I decided to wait maybe he'll tell me. He asked me to follow him to his squad car and I complied and came out of the taxi. After I walked out of the taxi, I realized that I left my wallet on the seat, so I turned back instantly within a split second and grabbed my wallet.

As I turned back towards him the officer had drawn his pistol, with his finger on the trigger, he shouted, "drop your gun". His hands were trembling. I quickly dropped my wallet and asked, what gun? He said that I was very lucky that he almost hit the trigger, by now he realized he was just panicking for nothing, that I had no weapon. "Oh you thought I was reaching for a gun, and that's why you almost shot me", I said to him. "Do you know how many cops have been killed this way", he asked. "I don't know but if you have to shoot people because of your imagination, instead of reason then your job as a police officer is no longer public safety", I told him.

We sat down in the squad car and at that point I asked him what he stopped me for. He said I went through a red light, I told him that I only saw a yellow light when we both drove across the intersection, and that I did not see any red light. He however decided to warn me instead of issuing me a ticket. But the point of the story is that I came close to being shot obviously for a silly decision that I made to grab my wallet. I wondered if the officer followed departmental procedures when he drew his gun. When next you hear that an officer shot somebody for reaching for something that looked like a weapon, you now have a better understanding of how it happened. The mother of all dangers facing cab drivers is the possibility of being killed during a robbery. It is a real danger. No day goes by that I am not reminded of this danger. The following chapter shows that such fears are real.

Chapter 10

The Robbery And Shooting Of A Dear Friend

Chicago Cab drivers are not allowed to carry weapons, but even if they do, it does not guarantee their safety, for the simple reason that they are usually taken by surprise by a passenger that suddenly turns into a robber. How can anyone defend against a robber that puts a gun to the back of your head at point blank range? The story you will read in this chapter is about such a robbery. Very often in Chicago one listens to cab robbery and shooting, and for those of us along this line of work it serves as a reminder of the presence of such danger.

There is a possibility that a taxi driver may leave for work and never return alive. Drivers were being robbed and killed in Chicago by the dozens, prior to the introduction of the safety shield. The safety shield for the most part, acts as a psychological deterrent on the potential robber, but besides that factor, it does not offer them a full security. Despite the installation of the safety shield however, Chicago cab drivers are still robbed and killed, but the frequency is somewhat reduced.

One of my personal friends was killed while operating a taxi in Chicago prior to the introduction of the shield. It is a very sad story to remember. The day he was shot, was actually an off day for him, but he told me, he was going to the bank, to get some money to pay his lease at the Yellow cab company, where he worked. At that time, I was also driving for the Yellow Cab Company as well, as an owner operator; one of those expressions that gives you a feeling of control, but from a financial standpoint, the only person who makes money out of such arrangement in the Yellow cab company. For a weekly fee of about four hundred and fifty dollars the owner operator gets a new or used yellow taxi.

Part of the arrangement is that the owner operator undertakes the repair and maintenance of the vehicle-a very costly option for the driver. The only service the owner operators get, is the yellow cab prestige, a free car wash from the company, and radio dispatch. But anyway in order not to loose tract of the shooting of my friend, I shall leave that subject and focus on the robbery story.

I had just met Zubi as we called him about six months before his fatal shooting, and our friendship was just developing. We have had conversations about the dangers of Taxi work in Chicago, but there is always that feeling that such tragedies would not befall on us. At that point, Zubi had just separated from his wife and was just trying to put his life back together. I would describe him as a hard working and bright young man with a lot of unfulfilled goals in life.

Details of what happened following his shooting were confusing. There were speculations, that he was set up for that crime. On his way to pay his lease after withdrawing money from the bank, he branched off to see some people he knew. Along the way, he picked up a fare to the South shore area of the city. His passenger was a young male, and Zubi did not know the evil going through his mind. The trip continued until his attacked reached the point where his evil act would be executed. His passenger was immediately transformed into a robber. He asked Zubi to pull over, and pulled out a gun and pointed it to Zubi's head. Whatever transpired between him and his attacker is unknown. It is unclear if Zubi put up any resistance or not, but he was shot several times on the back of his head and neck area, in an execution style, at a point blank range. This clearly suggests that Zubi could not have put up resistance, since he was shot at the back of his head. He was rushed to St Anthony's hospital in Lincoln Park, where he underwent an emergency surgery, for his wounds.

After the surgery I saw him with other friends and he was able to speak a few words, he cautioned us, to be very careful when driving taxi in Chicago, because there are many dangers out there. He warned us to pay attention to people we pick up. In fact, it was a very emotional encounter that I had with him, as this young man full of life and energy, lay helpless on a hospital bed. After the first surgery, a second one was scheduled, because of the complications of the first, but he did not recover from it, he lapsed into comma, and never came out of it. Perhaps if the safety shield was installed in his cab, may be he would still be alive, but who knows.

Majority of the cab drivers in Chicago leave the safety shield open while passengers are riding behind, thereby defeating the purpose. I understand why this happen; the Chicago cab patrons do not like the mandatory safety shield; many think they are being imprisoned in the back of the taxi. I remember a case where a passenger who stopped me, simply did not enter my taxi, telling me that the shield is too uncomfortable.

Others think that the idea of locking them behind the taxi driver simply make them look like criminals, which they are not. When the shield was first introduced, I usually tell my passengers when they ask me about it, that it was not installed for them, the good passengers, but to keep the hooligans out, usually that satisfies them. But some passengers think the shield is uncomfortable, because it does not allow them to straighten their legs. To address that problem the City of Chicago introduced mini vans, just the other day, I had a passenger who bypassed the minivan ahead of me, on the taxi line at the newly completed House of Blues Hotel. I told her that the minivan was the next in line, but she told me the mini-vans are not comfortable, particularly when the driver applies a sudden brake.

Taxi crime went down with the introduction of the safety shield but if one cab driver is murdered on the job, as far as I am concerned, it is one too many. Cab service is extremely vital for any city, they help to facilitate business and tourism, and if you ask the Chicago commuters, they would tell you what a typical commute for them would be like without the luxury of inexpensive taxi service in the City.

There are other dangers associated with taxi driving in the windy city, chances of the driver being killed in an accident in their taxi is among those dangers, but traffic related stress, is also among the greatest challenges for the taxi driver, hopefully, these stories would give you the reader a true understanding of the difficulties and challenges which your taxi driver has to deal with on a day to day basis.

Chapter 11
The Taxi Driver's Ordeal

Taxi work as simple as it may appear is not for everyone. When a friend of mine asked me about the job I simply told him all the pros and cons of the job. I informed him that unless his tolerance level was high, and he has a considerable amount of patience to deal with the public, he should for all intents and purposes consider other jobs. He assured me that he could handle the job. At least I justified my conscience as a good friend by being truthful with him.

Nothing has shaped my understanding of society as taxi work. I have been able to see society from a different perspective since I took up this work. I have met the rich, the poor, celebrities, homeless, beggars, politicians, and basically people from all aspects of life. I have learnt over my cab driving years that human beings are inherently egocentric in nature. Each person or group basically think they are socially and culturally more advanced than others, when in fact no one is better than the other, at least from a biological point of view. Individuals look different from one another basically because of color pigmentation, which is the result of environmental evolution process.

But this phenomenon has a historical origin. The Chinese once considered non-Chinese as barbarians. German nationalism under Adolph Hitler led to the annihilation of millions of people during the Second World War. The average taxi passenger looks down on the taxi driver, while the society at large assigns a little value if any to the taxi occupation. But as dumb as cab drivers are, passengers are ready however to trust their life and safety to them. This is a contradiction in itself.

To make matters worse, the average taxi driver in Chicago is relatively a recent emigrant. Aliens whether "legal" or "illegal" are generally regarded as un-American. Aliens have accents, and speak differently than the rest of the population. Some people in Chicago think that some Chicago taxi drivers don't understand English, this may be rightly so, but I do think the problem is blown out of proportion. I was aware of these stereotyping problems when I took the job. Over the years, cab drivers that have been on the job for some time, eventually do accept the inevitable fact that people would naturally look down on them, as well as their occupation. The new taxi driver would however have a tougher time dealing with the problem. I have seen many situations where pedestrians spit on the taxi driver. Some passengers may throw-up inside the taxi, and not even show a remorse for that.

I explained all these realities to my friend Peter. Peter decided that he could handle it, so he moved his family to Chicago and started a taxi-driving career in the windy city.

His first incident happened on his second day of his taxi career. Peter picked up his passenger from the Gold Coast neighborhood of the city. His passenger was heading to the Northwestern train station on the corner of Madison and Canal streets. As with most commuters in Chicago, this passenger was also running late.

So my friend was asked to hurry things up. When Peter got to the corner of Wacker and Madison streets, he encountered a long line of pedestrians crossing Wacker Street. His passenger reminded him, she was about to miss her train. Peter tries to make a wide right turn from the middle lane, but an unyielding pedestrian stood on his way motionless. As Peter tried to move away from her, she spat on the hood of his taxi. Peter soon pulled up to the train station and let his passenger off.

"This is nothing to disturb you", I assured Peter when he told me of his ordeal. "You should be happy she did not spit on your face," I added. Peter's next incident happened on a Saturday night. It involved the bar hopping teenagers. At about twelve midnight, Peter picked up a group of four young men from the Hunt club on Elm Street. They were going to Skokie, a suburb of Chicago. Three passengers sat behind, and one passenger sat in the front seat. About five minutes into the trip, Peter noticed that his front seat passenger was looking somewhat drowsy. A few moments later he fell asleep. The three passengers at the back seat started bragging to one another about how much beer they consumed at the bar where they had been drinking.

Meanwhile the front seat passenger was fast asleep, and was snoring fairly loudly. Suddenly he woke up and asked Peter to stop. Peter was driving on the middle lane of Lakeshore drive heading north. He managed to change lanes and pulled into the right lane. The front seat passenger grabbed his mouth with his two hands.

Before Peter could pull out into the curbside lane, this passenger through up on the dashboard of the taxi. It was a horrible scene Peter told me, as he puked directly into the air vent on the dashboard, contaminating the air vent system of the cab, as well as Peter's clothes. Peter had come to a complete stop by now, and he was momentarily speechless. This meant that his workday has finally come to an end. Peter's indignation stems from the fact that his passengers were not apologetic. In fact the guys at the back seat were having fun over the incident. One of the passengers actually told Peter that it was part of the job. Peter managed a small roadside clean up so as to enable him complete the fare.

He continued on the trip to Skokie and after he dropped his passengers off, he drove straight to the taxi office. He informed the dispatcher that he was dropping the taxi, because of the incident explaining the details to the Dispatcher. Peter went home. He took off for about one week, reflecting on his experience as a Chicago cab driver.

When Peter summoned up some courage, he went back to the taxi company and leased out another cab. For the next three weeks, things were fine, and he thought that things are now beginning to settle down for him. Well not for long before his next dilemma surfaced. It was a Halloween day and he took a group of young teenagers to an address on the far west side. Halloween nights are crazy in Chicago. Veteran drivers know neighborhoods to avoid on such nights, but new and inexperienced drivers often lack such experience. This is an experience that is very familiar to me because I have encountered such a problem few times.

When Peter got to his passenger's destination, his young passengers jumped out of the taxi and ran away into a nearby alley. The fare on the meter was about nine dollars. He turned around and decided to head back to the loop. He only traveled a few blocks when objects began landing on his taxi. Peter wondered what was happening. He pulled over to check it out.

About three more objects landed on the sides of the cab. He soon realized that some teenagers were throwing raw eggs at his taxi. As he tried to escape, one of the raw eggs landed squarely on his face, splashing raw eggs in all directions. Peter managed to drive the taxi away from the neighborhood straight back to the company where he leased the taxi. This incident effectively ended his taxi-driving career. This is the plight of cab drivers. I can assure you with a high degree of certainty that Peter's experience is all too familiar to many of the Chicago cabbies.

Chapter 12
Chicago's Back-seat Drivers

Many cab riders in Chicago live in the loop. Parking in the loop has become so expensive, that an average one-hour parking would cost between fifteen and twenty dollars. The Chicago Police ticket and tow cars sometimes within minutes, from the time such cars were packed. It is a big business for the city. City tow trucks are busy towing vehicles twenty-four hours a day. Each towed vehicle brings in about one hundred and fifteen dollars.

When insurance costs and car notes are factored in, it becomes highly expensive to own an automobile particularly if you live in the loop. Many residents of the loop therefore choose not to own cars. They rely on a pretty effective public transportation. The CTA Blue lines connect them to O'Hare international airport, while the Orange line goes to Midway airport.

The EL train connects the city in all directions, north from Howard and south to Ninety-fifth Street. There is also the Brown and the Green lines, helping to make transportation in Chicago much easier. Added to this are the Metra Trains, connecting most of the suburbs in Chicago to the loop. The Amtrak station has a terminal in the heart of the loop as well

The Greyhound bus terminal is also located in the loop. In addition, taxis and Airport express busses are also other transportation modes available to the residents of the loop. As a result, many of the loop residents do not need personal cars.

Because or the relatively in-expensive cab fares in Chicago, compared to other large cities like New York or Los Angeles, most of the loop residents use the taxi for their daily transportation needs. Many of these loop residents think they know the city more than the cab drivers, whom they reason, are new comers to their city.

Cab drivers refer to these residents as “back-seat drivers”. They are quick to get into the taxi and issue specific directions to the taxi-driver. It is okay for them to do that, after all the city taxi code also stated that “the passenger has the right to request any route they prefer”. The problem comes when something goes wrong, like road or bridge closure, or when there are accidents, creating back-ups on their preferred routes.

Some passengers do own up to the problem as their fault, but others would attempt to blame the taxi driver, for the decision the passenger made. The following story is about such a trip. The time was about four-thirty in the evening on a Thursday. My passenger emerged from the LaSalle street train station on the corner of LaSalle and Van Buren streets in the loop.

She jumped into the taxi and asked to be taken to North Michigan Avenue, near Chicago Avenue. I was facing west on Van Buren Avenue, and my intension was to take Van Buren to Franklin Avenue, to Orleans, to Chicago Avenue, connecting Michigan Avenue.

But before I could turn into Franklin Avenue, she asked me to keep straight, saying she would show me a better way to go. I said okay. Next question from her followed almost immediately, she asked, “How long have you lived in Chicago”? I said, five years madam. She told me this is her twenty-fifth year in Chicago. So what, I thought to myself, after all, I did not actually ask for that information. Such comparison was uncalled for I thought, but anyway the trip continued, and she gave me additional directions.

“Take a right on Jefferson Street, to Fulton Street”, she further said. At that moment, I knew the rest of the route, she was directing me to, but I still wanted her to continue to direct me. “Turn left on Clinton Street, and a right on Kinzie” she added. As soon as I turned right on Kinzie, the first problem manifested. There was a traffic sign warning, it read, “Bridge Out”.

When I saw the sign, I asked her what she wanted me to do next. She exclaimed. Damn! Followed by a four-letter “F” word. I said, madam no obscenities please. She asked me to turn around and take Halstead Avenue. We took Halstead Avenue to Chicago Avenue, she asked me to turn right on Chicago Avenue; unfortunately for her, the Chicago Bridge across the river was also closed to repairs.

The meter kept on ticking, by now the fare was already more than the normal fare to her destination. She was furious at that, asking me why did I not tell her that the Kinzie Bridge was closed. I told her that I had no idea that it was closed, and that I was relying on her twenty-five years experience to work for us. She turned her anger over to Mayor Daley, saying he is doing a terrible job, I asked how could he be doing a terrible job repairing the city infrastructure?

She asked for my suggestions at this point, I said her next option was Division Street, but the decision was up to her. I was careful not to take responsibility for the trip. Division Street was fine, but at this point a normal six-dollar fare had turned into nine dollars and more.

We finally got to her destination, the meter read ten dollars and some change, She grudgingly paid the fare. Her decision cost her an extra four dollars, and fifteen minutes more than the usual time such fare takes. As she left the taxi, I thanked her for showing me this short cut, informing her, that I would however stick to the one I knew. She smiled and I took off, a clear case of penny-wise pound-foolish.

Chapter 13
It's My Dog's Pizza

It was five o'clock on Sunday evening; I drove my cab down on Wells street looking for fares. The LaSalle Street Bridge across the Chicago River was closed due to the ongoing construction of the Lower Wacker drive. Since the closure of the LaSalle Street bridge, most of the traffic going from the near north areas to the loop used either Clark or Wells streets at that moment.

Three passengers at the corner of Wells Street and Ontario flagged me down. They were coming from the Ginos'Pizza restaurant, on the corner. Gino's is one of the deep-dish pizzas, fairly popular with tourists. I should add also, that local Chicago residents eat there as well, in addition to Giordano's, Pizzeria Due, and Pizzeria Uno, you have in between them the best of the famous deep dish Pizzas popular in Chicago.

Chicago's Popular Ginos Pizza, Where my passengers in this story were picked up from

My passengers entered my cab with a packed bag of extra pizza from Gino's restaurant. Two passengers sat at the back seat, and one sat in the front seat. How are you doing? One of the passengers inquired from me, I said fine, and "how are you gentlemen", I asked. All of them replied simultaneously in a fairly synchronized voice "fine"

They told me they were going back to the Hilton Towers hotel on south Michigan Avenue. I turned on the meter, and added a one-dollar charge for two extra passengers. The front seat passenger asked me what the one-dollar extra charge was for. This is usually a signal for cab drivers that the passengers are cheap. This also means that the driver if he is lucky would get a tip.

I explained to them that the city taxi rate requires an extra passenger to pay a fifty cent extra charge, and since there are two extra passengers, the extra charge was one dollar. There was no more confusion about the one dollar extra charge after my explanation. One of the back seat passengers said he was so stuffed up from the pizza they had at Ginos, it was a pretty good pizza he added. A second passenger concurred, but asked the passenger in front whether he remembered to take the left over pizza, and he replied, "yes"

He was also asked, what he would do with the left over pizza. He reminded his colleagues that he is scheduled to fly back home in about two hours, so he would carry the pizza home to his dogs. I thought at first that it was a joke, but soon I realized that the front passenger was actually serious about taking the pizza back home with him.

The back seat passengers suggested that he should pass on the left over pizza to the taxi driver. I gave the impression that I did not hear that suggestion, because he was not talking to me directly, but rather an expression of his free speech rights. All the three passengers were going back and forth arguing whether he should take that pizza back to his dog or not. As long as they did not offer me the pizza directly, I was comfortable having them run their mouths I imagined.

Usually cabdrivers do not respond to taxi conversations, unless the passengers asked them a direct question, or invites them to participate in the discursions. The city taxi course reminds drivers not to initiate conversations between them and the passengers, unless the passenger initiates one. Undoubtedly, this comes close to violating the freedom of speech clause of the U.S. Constitution, but cab drivers don't care any way.

Cab drivers are a bunch of uneducated and uninformed immigrants the city taxi bureau probably thinks, a topic I have previously addressed. So the fare continued towards the Chicago Hilton and Towers, which is the requested destination. One of the passengers on the back seat asked me if I like pizza, I said yes, I do eat pizza. I knew the direction he was heading, and I was going to help him get to that inevitable question which he is setting himself up to ask.

There was a little silence after I replied him that indeed I do like pizza. I overheard the second back seat passenger asking his colleague at the back if they should ask the driver if he wanted the pizza. I was not exactly sure what the answer was, but I was still anticipating that the question would eventually be put to me.

Meanwhile the front seat passenger was quiet, but soon he put his own question to me, he said, "Do you like Ginos pizza", I told him, that I love Ginos pizza, again giving them added impetus why they should pose that question to me sooner. I could have told him that, I don't like Ginos pizza, but I knew it could also end the conversation. I was simply curious to see where these questions would lead.

I was not exactly sure what my answer would be if and when such question was put to me, but I would let my instinct and reflex, guide me through this dilemma. At this point I was getting a little irritated over this ordeal, and my feeling was that whatever final question they may have, they should get it out now.

But not long after this thought came to me, the question soon came up. The passenger sitting directly behind me soon summoned up the courage and asked, "Would you like to have the left over pizza, it was not messed up or anything, we just could not finish it, and it was neatly packaged"?

By now increased adrenaline was flowing through me, I was charged up, the reason being that such question tends to dehumanize. The thought of the pizza meant for his dog being offered to me, was an insult as far as I am concerned, within split seconds, I contemplated what my reaction would be.

But I was not going to let my emotions overcome me, so I replied with a calm but ideological answer, I said, “sir, thank you for the offer, I have no desire for your leftover pizza, we, that live in Chicago do not take leftover pizza home, it belongs in the trash can, because I don’t even think it’s good enough for your dog either”.

There was some quiet in the taxi; the exuberant mood suddenly became subdued. My mind tells me that my reply was respectfully strong, I could have said tougher things, but once in a while the taxi driver remembers the lessons they were taught at the city-administered taxi-drivers’ course. The instructor tells you that you are an ambassador for the city, because the taxi-driver is the last impression for the tourist. This is more so because the taxi-driver is the first and last passenger that visitors in the city encounters. However, I could not wait much longer for these passengers to get out of town with their damned pizza.

One of the deficiencies of the city's taxi education course is that it does not adequately prepare the drivers on how to handle circumstances, such as the one I presented here.

There were no further conversations in the taxi between my passengers and me. I decided to turn on the fm radio. I tuned in my favorite station, wfmt 98.7; luckily there was a soothing classical performance on the station. It was one of my favorite pieces, Beethoven symphony no.3 in E flat major. I had memorized all of that, because I also have the CD at home. It was the Eroica symphony.

For the rest of the trip, every one in the taxi took refuge in Beethoven's music as I pulled into the Hilton and Towers Hotel on 700 block of south Michigan Avenue. Fare was about seven dollars and seventy cents, and my passengers disembarked, I was paid eight dollars, which included a thirty cents tip. But I knew, from the moment questions came up about the extra charge that my passengers were cheap. The front seat passenger walked straight to the nearest garbage can, near the entrance to the hotel, and tossed in the leftover pizza. He looked back at me, and I made an eye contact with him assuring him that I took notice. I gave him thumbs up signal, as I pulled off. I hope you the reader, by now have a measured sympathy for the trauma that cab drivers go through.

Chapter 14
Franklin/ Adams

Smoking in taxi is banned by a city of Chicago ordinance, yet smoking arguments are common between cab drivers and their passengers. Majority of the passengers obeys such a law, but often you come in contact with passengers who would assert their right to smoke in the taxi for the simple reason, that they are paying the fare.

Sometimes passengers would hold their cigarette, while walking down the taxi line, asking if they could smoke as a condition for taking that particular taxi. Some taxi drivers are smokers as well, although the majority of Chicago cab drivers are non-smokers. One day, I picked up a passenger from the Sears tower on Franklin Street. As soon as my passenger entered the taxi, he requested to be taken to an address on Lincoln Avenue. Usually smokers would ask if they could smoke or not, but for some reason, my passengers decided to just do it without asking if it was all right with me.

After he lit up his cigarette, I quickly drew his attention to the "No Smoking" sign posted inside the taxi. He asked me, why he could not smoke in this taxi, if he was going to pay me for the fare. I explained to him that there are several reasons why he could not. It is against a city of Chicago ordinance, which banned smoking in public vehicles. He argued that taxis are not public vehicles, that private individuals own them. I countered that while private individuals own taxis, the city grants them the Medallion to operate such a vehicle for the public use, and this enables the city to regulate the way and manner such vehicles should be operated and maintained.

I also explained to him that there is a conflict between his right to smoke and my right to breath a smokeless air, and if he does not like such a condition, then he should exercise his option not to take this particular taxi.

At this point he put out the cigarette, but was obviously unhappy with that. Few minutes after that he asked me, “Where are you from”? Considering the context the question was asked, I ignored the question. He repeated the question, this time in a louder voice, I told him that I live in Calumet City, obviously not the answer he was looking for, because my accent is not typically a Midwestern accent. I knew it was not an end to his inquiry, so I was expecting another question, which he soon asked. “How long have you lived in Calumet City”? He inquired, I replied “seven years”.

I was certain his intention was to find out what country I emigrated from, but I was not going to help him get to this point. "Before Calumet City which other place did you live in" he again asked me, "Atlanta Georgia" I told him, but I also indicated to him that I was not interested in his line of questions, which were increasingly personal in nature.

At this point we were approaching North Avenue and LaSalle intersection he instructed me to drive a little faster as he was running late. A red light on the corner of Lincoln Avenue and Clark soon caught us and I stopped, waiting for the green light.

Suddenly my passenger bolted from the taxi without paying me. He walked across the Park in the direction of the Lincoln Park Zoo. I thought momentarily if I should just forget about him and head back to the loop. Another thought directed me to pursue him. I decided to do the later; for one thing I knew his destination, if he did not fool me with a wrong address. I also knew the point where he could possibly come out from the park. So I decided to go to this point and wait for him. I waited for him at the corner of Fullerton Avenue and Lincoln Park West, and eventually I saw him walking at a distance. Unluckily for him there was a patrolling Police car along the Fullerton Avenue, and I flagged the officers down and explained to them what happened.

They drove up to him and I walked up to them as well. The Police asked him for his identification, he handed it to them. They also asked him if he was a passenger in my taxi, and surprisingly my passenger denied that he ever hired my taxi. The Police asked me for the address where I was going to drop him off, and I told them. It matched the address on his identification, which he gave to the Police. The Police asked him to pay me for the total fare, which at that time included all the waiting time. He claimed he had no money with him.

The Police told him that they would take him to jail if he did not pay for the fare. At this point he knew they meant business. He asked if he could go to the nearest cash station to get money. The Officers asked me if it was okay with me, and I said fine. We then drove to the cash station near Lincoln and Fullerton where he withdrew money and paid me the total of eighteen dollars.

At that point he got his identification back from the police and I thanked the officers for their help. My passenger headed north on Lincoln Avenue, while I drove back in the opposite direction, towards the loop.

Chapter 15
Jackson/Canal

Chicago is a very lively city. It is an interesting place to live, work and play. The only requirement for residency in the City is your ability to endure the punishing winter storms which would drive you crazy, but don't worry this only lasts for about six months of the year! As a Taxi driver, I see the best and worst of humanity. Every time I tell my friends that taxi job is a lazy man's job, I usually get into a prolonged argument, but the fact is that if you can drive a car, and you have a little common sense, which most human beings do, you could be a taxi driver. The only other requirement is your ability to cope with the overwhelming traffic conditions that sometimes may test your ability to maintain calm under tough situations that challenges you to act otherwise.

What about safety you may ask? Well there is nothing like safety anywhere, even in your home. But I do agree with those who say that Taxi job is the most dangerous occupation in America. I discussed the question of safety for the cab driver, in past chapters, it is nonetheless a serious problem, and I do not have any intension to downgrade the issue here.

The story for you here is not about safety or robbery related, it is a story of survival in the turf " hoods" in Chicago. In case I threw you off guard with the word " hoods", don't worry it is simply a gang abbreviation of "neighborhood". But here is my story; I just picked up a passenger from the Union Station in downtown Chicago going to 5300 block of Washington Avenue.

Many cab drivers would not accept fares to hoods like this one. But the dilemma with this situation is that the City of Chicago recently passed a law mandating that cab drivers could not discriminate against fare destinations in Chicago. This law simply means that a cab driver must pick up passengers regardless of their destinations.

But I picked up my passenger regardless of the fact that the neighborhood was a rough one. To make matters worse, my passenger opened up a conversation asking me how much the fare would amount to. I gave him an estimate of about fifteen dollars. We entered the I-290W. When passengers ask questions about fare estimates, followed by another question on the route the driver plans to take, it is a warning signal to the driver about potential trouble.

But my worries soon melted away when my passenger told me that he was just paroled from the prison, and he was going back home, after serving four years. Well I reasoned that perhaps the safest passenger, could be a paroled inmate, the reason are two fold.

The thrill of getting back home for the first time in four years is greater than the thought of committing another crime, and secondly, when individuals are going home from prison, they are truly unarmed. The potential for trouble from this passenger is low I reasoned.

Eventually we arrived at his home, but he needed to borrow additional two dollars to complete the fare, I asked him not to worry about that, so he paid the fare and I turned back wishing him well.

I pulled out and headed down to the expressway through Cicero Avenue. A middle-aged lady, hailed me down, and asked me to take her to the loop area.

She came into the taxi and sat down. I asked her to give me a specific address and she replied "State and forty-second Street". She need not tell me anymore, I knew the rest about the neighborhood, it was another tough one, but I was familiar with the area so I proceeded with the trip. This was the Robert Taylor Homes, a tough housing project on the Southside.

I turned the meter on and accelerated off on the trip. My passenger told me that she was just robbed of her purse, and gold chains. I replied, how much money did you loose, obviously a question to find out if she had any money left to pay for the fare. She started laughing, I asked what was funny, she replied that her boyfriend asked her to buy a joint, {Marijuana} a six pack of malt liquor, and three- park of condoms. "What a deadly combination", I said to her.

Do you have any idea what he is going to do with those items, I jokingly inquired. She laughed.

She further told me that she had just bought the joint, and the condoms, and was on the way to the liquor shop, when a man with a knife walked up to her and demanded her purse. She quickly handed him her wallet, which also contained the condoms and the joint. The robber snatched her fake gold chains and ran into an alley.

I asked her how much money was in her wallet; she said "only eight dollars." But she quickly added that she had another fifty dollars hidden away. The robber made away with the joint, a pack of condom, eight dollars in cash, and a fake gold chain. The rest of her money was safe, my passenger told me. At that point, I concluded that I knew where the rest or her money was hidden, since it is common for some women to hide.their money under their bra in tough neighborhoods.

As a city taxi driver, over the years of driving around, you begin to develop some psychological profile of the character of some neighborhoods. My previous experiences with Robert Taylor Homes are centered on two incidents that happened to me there. In both occasions, my passengers ran away without paying for the fare, knowing that nobody would chase them into those projects.

Chicago's Robert Taylor Housing Project, where my passenger was dropped off

So I was aware of that possibility, but in this case, she is a woman, and generally, women don't do things like that. Eventually we got to her destination and I pulled over. The total fare was twelve dollars, as she took notice.

I waited for her to pay me so I can move on, but she was moving from one side of the seat to the other. I asked her what was the problem and she said "nothing", that she was simply reaching for her money. I became curious about what was going on, for one thing I was not going to seat by indefinitely, so I attempted to look across the bullet proof partition, but she asked me not to look at her, her statement actually increased my suspicion.

I adjusted the rear-view mirror so as to maintain a close look at her movements, but I could only see her upper body, from her chest up, and meanwhile, her hands were out of view. I was increasingly getting frustrated so I decided to find out what she was doing. I put my head across the bullet proof partition, so as to have a clear view of her lower body.

"My goodness, what are you doing"? I asked her. She replied, "You want to be paid don't you"? "Yes of course" I said. I could not believe what I saw but I will let you draw your own conclusion. She had just pulled out a small plastic from her genitals. I mean this happened before my own eyes. She unwrapped the plastic and brought out a $50 note and said to me, "here is your money".

I told her that I have no change and pointed to the sign displayed behind the back seat, that "driver does not carry change in excess of twenty dollars".

Meanwhile I knew that I had enough money on me to change the fifty dollar note, but under no circumstance would I touch the money she pulled out from her genitals, so we reached an impasse. I would not let her leave without paying me. I also realized that the law is on her side so I tried to work out a compromise.

I suggested to her that I am willing to drive her to the nearest store at my expense to get change, she agreed and I drove down on State street to the liquor store. It worked as the unsuspecting cashier at the liquor store, not knowing where the almighty dollar came from, took the fifty dollar note from her.

She came back to the car and paid me as I dropped her off.

As she walked away, I told her that I now know how the robber only got eight dollars from her. She smiled and walked away. You have to love this wonderful city on the lake!

Chapter 16
Staging Area At O'Hare

Waiting time at the airport ranges from one to two hours. During the waiting time so many activities take place at the staging area. The staging area is a world of its own. There is no place to see the diversity of the City of Chicago better than there. Taxi drivers from well over fifty countries interact with one another. Such interaction is largely based on ethnicity.

Hundreds of Taxis line up at the O'Hare Airport Taxi stand, patiently waiting for their turns

So many different languages are spoken, from Afghan Pashtun, to Swahili of South Africa. From Creole to Yoruba, the O'Hare staging area is a melting pot of world's cultural diversity. On one area, a group of Ibo drivers from Nigeria are exchanging views about politics of their home country. A few feet away, Chinese drivers are gathered, conversing in their local language. Ten yards away I saw five Indian Sikhs recognized by their headband, chatting. Poles, Yugoslavs, Czechs, Romanians, Pakistanis, Algerians, Ashantis and, Haitians are all present.

All kinds of music fill the air. Indian and Pakistani music as well as Yoruba juju music are among the loudest. One African American driver was enjoying an African American gospel music, and next to his car, an Egyptian cabbie was listening to the Islamic readings recited by a local Imam.

On the far west corner, a group of Moslems were bowing their heads in a synchronized fashion in a prayer session. In fact the O'Hare airport administrators have just added a multi-use facility for such activities.

Some cabbies are busy playing cards or chess games. In the mist of these activities are announcements from the taxi dispatchers blazing through the loudspeakers. Instructions from the Airport rental car return office across the street are also heard. But "the mother of all the loud noises" occurs at one-minute intervals. It is the deafening aircraft engines, so loud that the deaf may hear it. The staging area sits at the end of the airport runways.

A fast food restaurant is also located at the O'Hare staging area. A well-connected businessman was granted a concession stand, displacing the ethnic food vendors. Some cab drivers think it was unfair to drive away the small food vendors, replacing them with a mediocre fast food restaurant.

Soon it is time for cabbies to go down to the terminal to pick up fares. This is the time that every cabbie is waiting for. There are five pick-up locations- Terminal 1 {mostly preferred by drivers}, Terminal 2, Terminal 3A, Terminal 3B {Delta}, and Terminal 5 {Mostly hated pick up point} Most cab drivers like to pick up from terminal 1 for two reasons; it is the busiest terminal, and the longest point to all fare destinations. On the other hand, Terminal 5 is the shortest point to all fare destinations; in addition, it is the pick up point for all international arrivals. International passengers do not generally give tips. Cab drivers avoid terminal 5, because it is the slowest terminal and it is the arrival terminal for the dreaded Mexican flights. Not only that Amigos do not tip, they also live closest to the airports.

Section II
Taxi Stories

Chapter 17
Engagement That Never Was

He hailed me down at the corner of Clark Street and Lincoln Avenue, requesting me to wait for him, to pick up his luggage from the hotel lobby. The hotel was the Days Inn at the Gold Coast neighborhood of Chicago. I pulled up, and opened the trunk.

Soon he emerged from the hotel, carrying a brief case and a small luggage, I took the luggage and placed it inside the trunk. He entered the taxi, and instructed me to take him to the United Airlines at O'Hare International airport. He inquired how long the trip would take; I gave him an estimate of about forty minutes to an hour.

I turned the meter on and set out on the trip. As soon as I entered North Avenue, He said to me, "would you believe what happened to me," I said "what, are you okay", I curiously inquired, he said yes, that his problem was nothing that serious. He introduced himself to me as Ron, and told me, his fiancée just dumped him. What was the problem I asked him?

Here is the rest of his story. Ron flew in from Los Angeles to see his fiancée; he called Lizzy on Friday night. He said he has dated

Lizzy for about two years. Lizzy is a successful hair stylist and owned a beauty salon in Lincoln Park. Ron went out with Lizzy on Friday night after his arrival from Los Angeles.

Along the way Lizzy picked up two of her friends, Audrey and Angela to join them in a quiet celebration of what would have been their engagement party. They had lots of fun at the bar and they visited about three bars. Ron said he was wasted {drunk}. They came back home about two o'clock on Saturday morning, but the problem was they needed some more booze at home. Lizzy does not have any more booze in her apartment.

Angela remembers she has a few bottles of champagne left, she suggested that Lizzy should take her to her apartment on Fullerton avenue to pick up the drinks. Lizzy decided it was a good idea, and left with Angela, leaving Ron and Audrey in the apartment.

Ron did not realize that this was a test of his fidelity in the making. When Lizzy and Angela got to the car, Lizzy stayed behind and Angela drove off creating the impression that both Lizzy and Angela drove away together.

Meanwhile Lizzy made her way back to her apartment through the back door. Ron and Audrey were not aware of that because the music was fairly loud, so none of them heard any noise when Lizzy entered the apartment. Ron started making advances towards Audrey, and he told me that Audrey welcomed such advance.

Their plan was for a quick romance right there in Lizzy's living room. Ron walked to the light switch, and if only he looked near the closet he would have seen Lizzy hiding, but he did not, so he dimmed the lights in the living room. But Lizzy would not allow the act to get started. If she had waited for another ten minutes, she would have caught Ron and Audrey in the act itself. Lizzy waited for a few minutes and walked to the light switch. She turned the light back to its brightest. Ron and Audrey were caught red handed. Ron said he was kissing Audrey when the lights came back. He was surprised when he saw Lizzy.

Audrey was not part of the plot. Ron and Audrey could not believe what happened, and Lizzy was so angry that she carried Ron's briefcase and luggage and threw them out of the window. Ron tries to calm Lizzy down by apologizing and re-assuring Lizzy of his love, with no luck. Audrey saw what was unfolding, and hit the door. Ron pleaded with Lizzy to give him a second chance but his pleas fell on a deaf ear.

Ron said he left the apartment to pack up his things that were tossed out of the window. Audrey meanwhile had vanished. Ron ended up at the Days Inn in Lincoln Park. Luckily for Ron, he had a return ticket back to Los Angeles. He said he was running short of money, I asked him if he had enough for the fare, and he said yes.

I told him his story was good for a TV movie. But it drew no sympathy from me for some reason. Ron's explanation was based on the point that he was so drunk, but I was not moved at all. We soon arrived at the airport terminal. He paid me for the fare, and I bid him farewell. I was surprised for two things, that anyone could be this stupid, and even have the guts to tell this story to a third party. Ron thinks he could still convince Lizzy to give him another chance, all I could wish him is good luck.

As Ron walked away, I had one more look at him, obviously, he did not realize what a big fool he made of himself.

Chapter 18
In Search Of Hookers

On another day, a young passenger got into the taxi, heading to a bar on Rush Street, obviously he had too much drink, and at the same time a little horny. He told me that he was going fishing tonight. I obviously misunderstood him, as naïve as I was, I asked him why would he go fishing this late at night. He had a prolonged laugh; but explained to me that he meant fishing for hookers. I said, "excuse me". He asked me to assist him in finding some hookers, and further asked me to take him to the spot where hookers hang out.

I told him that I had no slightest idea, reason being that City ordinances forbid cab drivers from helping passengers solicit for hookers. He said some other cab driver told him he should go to North avenue, I said "sir if you want me to take you to North avenue, as your destination I would gladly do that for you, but I do not know where you can find hookers".

The time was about ten o'clock on a Friday evening; he decided that I should take him to North Avenue instead. I dropped him off at North Avenue and Kingsbury streets and he paid me off. Well he was right about that destination being popular for hookers, I was certain he would not find any hookers at that time however. He may have a better chance if he waited until after midnight. I was not going to give him any suggestions any way. I drove down North Avenue for about a mile, but decided to turn back and head back to the loop.

To my surprise this guy was standing on the spot where I dropped him off, in a company of a lady. They flagged me down as I approached them. The lady walked towards me, and greeted me. She asked me how much I would charge for an hour lease. I asked her where they were going to. She said no place in particular, just to drive along the lakefront. I told her I would charge them thirty dollars an hour. They entered the taxi, and we drove towards lakeshore drive.

I had my thoughts about their plans, but I wanted to see if they would be silly enough to try such a thing inside the taxi. The time then was about 10.30 pm. We drove into lakeshore drive heading south. When I approached Oak and Michigan Avenue exit she unzipped his pants. I looked at the rear view mirror, and made an eye contact with the lady passenger. She was seated on the right side of the back seat. She told me that she likes the way I drive. I told her thanks. This was a decoy I thought because something else was on her mind at that particular time. Meanwhile the male passenger was out of view, because he was seated directly behind me. The trip continued south on lakeshore drive. Every few seconds I looked at the rear view mirror, watching the lady passenger's suspicious activities. Each time I looked at the mirror, I noticed she was watching me as well.

I asked her again how far down on lakeshore drive should we go, before turning back. She asked me to go to 57th street exit, then turn into the Museum of Science and Industry parking lot, and then head back towards the loop. When we passed 31st street exit, her head was out of view. I had to see what was about to unfold on the back seat. I quickly pulled over, and looked through the partition window. Yes my theories were correct. She was about to begin a blowjob on the back seat of my taxi.

What are doing? I asked her. She zips this guy's pant up. The male passenger was a little embarrassed. I told her, she knows better than that. Such an act could land us in a big trouble. I would not allow such a thing under no condition. The male passenger offered me a twenty-dollar tip if I ignored what they were doing at my back seat. I assured him that my taxi would not be used for such activities.

The lady asked me to take them to a budget motel on the corner of Michigan and Twenty-sixth Street. We continued south on lakeshore to Oakwood exit. I dropped them off at the requested motel and they paid me off.

When I first told this story to cab driver friend of mine, he told me I was missing out great opportunities for greater tips, and I inquired, “What do you mean”? He explained that such activities happen inside taxis all the time. I said what about the city ordinance forbidding such activities. He told me that some of those city Aldermen had mistresses for services like that. Obviously an exaggeration there I thought.

My friend asked me how much tip did I get from my passengers, I said none, he told me that’s exactly what I’ll get for playing by the rules. I assured him that I have no regrets over that, because some activities belong in the bedroom, and not in a taxi.

Chapter 19
When Men Are Drunk

Another story that will thrill you is what happened on Saturday morning at the "Drink Night club", near the intersection of Halstead Avenue and Fulton streets. It was the stage for another drunk story. The "Drink" is a busy nightclub fairly popular for bar hoppers in Chicago, drawing a lot of its crowd from both tourists and local residents alike.

It was about four o'clock in the morning, almost closing time for bars in Chicago. The "Drink" is among some bars with extended closing hours on Saturdays, with a five o'clock limit, and many taxis were parked on the queue, waiting for the crowd, about to come out. On the other side of the street was a police car, with an officer sitting inside it.

A young man obviously very drunk staggered out of the bar and walked towards my cab. I said oh no, I was not going to deal with him this late in the morning. Some of the most difficult fares I have undertaken involved a drunken person. By then I was the first cab on the line. This guy walked close to the driver's window where I sat, and asked me, “Where the hell am I?” I was not going to prolong this situation so I quickly told him he was at the “Drink” bar at the corner of Halstead and Fulton Avenues in downtown Chicago, hoping, that would be the end of it.

I was wrong, he followed up with another question, “How the hell did I get here”, this second question actually was a little more irritating than the first, for one thing the language as well the way he asked the questions were inappropriate, but as a reflex action I answered him in the same manner, saying to myself, what was good for the geese was also good for the gander. I asked him back, “How the hell would I know “.

He asked one more question, “Where the hell is the closest bath room?” he inquired, I pointed at the bar behind him, whose name ironically was “Drink”. He said to me “No I don’t want any more drink, thinking that I was referring to “drink” as in beer. I decided not to answer any more questions from him, if he asked another one, since there was no point, if he could no longer remember that the bar, he just left, was called “Drink”.

The next thing I saw, was this fellow staggered across, to the other side of the street, next to the front window of the police squad car.

The police officer sitting inside the car watched as well. I said in my mind, what is this guy going to do now, but the answer to my question was quick to follow. Obviously he did not see the officer in the patrol car.

He unzipped his pants, and pulled out his penis, and urinated right next to the police. It was one of those nights that Chicago lived up to its name of "Windy City", it was a breezy and windy early morning, and the first thought that came to my mind was the possibility that the wind may have helped to spray his urine in the direction of the open police car.

As soon as he finished with his piss, the officer came out of the squad car, and you know when an officer pulls his belt and pants upwards, that he means business. Unfortunately for me it was time for my next fare as another passenger entered my taxi, so I was unable to see the story play itself out, but your imagination is probably right in reaching a conclusion on what the officer did. Chicago is a city where unsolicited drama plays out on your face, whether you like it or not.

Chapter 20
She Was Drunk Too

One night, a young woman about 23 years of age was led out of a nightclub near the intersection of Chicago Avenue and Halstead Street. The club was called Kaboom nightclub, which was later, closed down by city authorities for some violations.

The time was about 1.30 am on Saturday night. The security men held her on both hands as they approached my taxi. Are you available? One of the security guards asked me. I said yes and they opened the door of the taxi and helped this young woman into the taxi.

They passed on an address to me in the Lincoln Park area of the city. As soon as my passenger entered the taxi and sat down, I knew that she had too much alcohol and usually that presents a problem because once such passengers get a little comfortable they immediately fall into a deep sleep. True enough, my worst fears were soon confirmed, because three minutes after she entered the taxi, she started sleeping.

I resorted to my strategy of engaging such passengers in a conversation as a way of keeping them awake throughout the trip. This strategy was effective for another five minutes after which my questions to her were unanswered. I knew at that point that I had lost the battle, so I left her to enjoy her night sleep, as I wondered if I was going to succeed in waking her up. What would I do if she failed to wake up became an immediate concern.

Twenty minutes later, I pulled up to an address given to me by the guards, I told her we have reached her home. There was no reply, I increased my voice with a second announcement, but was met with silence. I did not know what to do next, the first thought was to go to the apartment and knock at the door, but it was apparent to me that it would not work because there were about eight units in the building. I would be knocking on all the units, and announcing the problem to everyone who lives there, if I decided to use that tactic. I momentarily decided against that option.

Meanwhile the trip had taken more than the usual time that such trips normally take without an end in sight, and my frustrations had begun to mount.

The next thought was to call the police, and wait for them to arrive, but usually such weekend nights, the police responds to more calls, meaning more waiting time, the dilemma continued but my patience was thinning out. I said to her in an ever louder voice, "Hello miss", but my screams fell on a deaf ear. Should I head back to the night club I thought, that would mean loosing the fare and all the time already spent on the trip, but if it boiled down to that, I was willing to cut my losses. That would mean over one hour of my time. Well I decided to notify my company's radio dispatch personnel, thinking the problem would be resolved faster that way. It was not a good idea because my dispatcher ended up asking me, what were the options, call the police she inquired? Realizing that this process would take a longer time to complete, I decided to drive to the police station myself.

Half way to the police station, my passenger woke up after a series of successive hiccups. She looked to the left and to the right, and was surprised to find herself inside my taxi. She inquired from me how she got into my taxi. Suddenly I had some explanations to make. Well young lady I called her, "do you remember ever going to the Kaboom nightclub"? She said "yes", "well that was where I picked you up". I explained further to her, that she was so drunk that the security guards decided to send her out of the bar. At this point she realized what happened. She then asked me how much further are we to her home? a few blocks I said. I took the next turn and dashed back to her place, luckily we made it there before she fell asleep again. The fare was twice the normal fare and I was not going to spend more time on the trip, so I told her to pay me half of the amount on the meter.

She said I took a longer route to her apartment, because she never paid that amount before, I thanked God this ordeal was finally over.

Chapter 21
My Passenger Ends Up In The Hospital

The story with this drunken passenger is the worst of all my drunken passenger stories. I was totally frustrated and had no other choice but take the steps that eventually landed him in the hospital. The decision was made in his best interest. This guy was simply out of it. I picked him up at the corner of Division and Wells street in the Gold Coast area.

Two other vacant cabs ahead of me had avoided picking him up. He was barely walking straight. He was dragging two bags with him as well. He stopped me, and I pulled over. I don't know why I stopped, because my experiences with drunken passengers are not good. I am sure it was the same reason that the two vacant cabs ahead of me passed him by. His facial expression was a testament to his drunken state. He managed to drag his two bags inside the taxi and sat down on top of one of them, bumping his head hard as he entered the taxi. Okay, he is now seated inside the taxi, too late for me to reject the fare; I was going to take my chances.

"Where are you going to"? I asked him.

"Palatine Illinois" he told me.

"What is the address?" I asked.

"Highway 53 and Rand road" he replied. That is not specific enough, I thought.

"Sir can you tell me the address of your house"? He thought for a few seconds, and said nothing. Obviously he had forgotten his home address, not a good sign at all.

"This is a long fare, do you have enough money to pay for this fare"? I inquired from him. "How much is the fare"? He asked.

"About seventy five dollars" I estimated.

He dipped his hands into his pocket and gave me sixty-five dollar deposit. The rate to Palatine from the loop is meter and half. But I took the deposit anyway and turned the meter on.

"Where are you coming from"? I asked

"I was just released from the jail at the Midway airport", he told me.

"What did you do"? I inquired." Because I called a flight attendant a nigger" Explaining further that he was traveling from Albuquerque New Mexico to see his parents who live in Palatine.

He also told me he was born in Palatine and grew up there before he moved to New Mexico. “Why would you insult the flight attendant that way, what did he do to you”? “Nothing, he is just a nigger and fag” “Are you prejudiced?” I asked him. “I don’t know,” he told me. I was perplexed that he would be that prejudiced against minorities, knowing quite well that he is a minority as well.

When his flight arrived at the Midway airport, he was handcuffed and locked up for about seven hours. That was as much conversation as we had before he fell asleep for the first time. I woke him up instantly to ask for his address again, because experience has shown me, that as drunk as this guy was, the chances of waking him up, if he slept for a while may be small. But he still did not remember his parent’s address. He told me that he would show me the way, when we exit from the highway.

I warned him that if I don’t succeed in waking him up, that I would drop him up at the police station.” I hate those bastards,” he said, he slept again. I decided to leave him alone. I had done my best I thought. Soon he began to snore. The taxi was vibrating as he snored. I continued on I-90 exiting on Il 53 as he directed me.

Few more miles on Il 53, I saw Rand road exit, where he told me to exit. I exited and got to the end of the ramp and pulled over. I call him, “Sir, Sir, Sir” There was no response. “This is Rand road exit”, I told him but he snored louder and louder. I started to bang on the taxi door, hoping he would get up. I turned the radio so loud thinking it may do the trick, but nothing worked. “Is this guy still breathing I wondered”. I held his hands and felt a pulse. What should I do next? I drove two more blocks to a White Hen Pantry on the corner and pulled into the parking lot. I went into the store, and asked the attendant to call the police for me. He asked me what the problem was, and I told him.

He dialed the Palatine Police and gave me the phone handle. I requested for a police officer. Five minutes later the first police car arrived. The officer approached me and asked, “What’s the matter”? My passenger just can’t wake up. Has he been drinking? The officer asked “too much drink” I told him.

“Where did you pick him up,” the officer inquired, also following up with a second question.” Where is he going”? “Palatine” I told the officer.

"Any address"? The police asked further. "Just Rand road he told me" I replied.

Soon a second officer pulls up. The first officer briefed him.

Both officers approached the scene. Officer A raised my passenger's arm. There were all kinds of gang tattoos on his arm. The officers talked for a few seconds. He was a member of a particular gang, one of the cops said. They pulled his shirts up, to expose his chest. Some more gang tattoos were exposed. I observed some tattoos on his body as well. I saw a tattoo of a human heart with a spear piercing it, a gun and a picture of a naked woman. What do these symbols represent? I wondered. These are weird signs I thought.

The officers monitored his breathing rate. He was breathing very slowly. One of the officers reached for my passenger's wallet to see his identification. They called him by his name hoping that it would awaken him up. The second officer slipped a hand glove on and started shaking my passenger, while he called his name. He did not wake up either.

At that point I started wondering if my passenger had lapsed into a comma. Two fire rescue trucks soon arrived at the scene. They were also briefed on what was going on. One fire fighter asked me a question he thought was funny. He said “Cabbie what did you do to him” “Sir” I replied “this is not funny”.

The Rescue Squad checked his heart rate again. He was still breathing. They also failed to wake him up as well. An ambulance was requested. What if this guy fails to get up, I wondered. Ten minutes later, an ambulance arrived at the scene. Two guys rushed to the scene holding stretchers. They asked the officers a few questions.

“Has he been drinking”? A second ambulance crew asked. “Way too much drink” an officer said. One of the ambulance crew ran back to the ambulance. He took something that looked like a cotton swab, but I was not sure. Whatever that substance was, it was obviously an irritating substance. He inserted it into my passenger’s nose. My passenger reacted by slapping the hands of the EMS crew. He got up and looked around for a while.

Then he did a strange thing, my passenger reached for something. I took cover behind the taxi. He brought out a small bag, opened it and gave the police a twenty-dollar bill. The police asked me if he had paid me. “He did but he has a balance” I said “How much balance”? The officer inquired” “I am not going to worry about that” I told him. They gave him his money back. He was acting weird. My passenger was again asked where he was going to, he still did not remember his parent's address. The address on his identification was his New Mexico residence.

The EMS crew brought the stretcher closer. They loaded his bags into the ambulance. My passenger was carried on the stretcher into the ambulance as well. It was not only alcohol, one EMS crew said; he may have overdosed on something. "We will take him to the emergency room to check him up. The police asked me to go. I had used up two extra hours for the trip. I decided to go home. The two cabbies that avoided him were right. I should have done the same. But thank goodness it's over at last. This is a crazy job indeed.

Chapter 22
A Daring Escape From Genital Mutilation

One of the interesting aspects of the taxi driver's work is the degree to which some passengers may open up their life story to them. Some passengers are eager to open up a conversation with the cab driver. Very often we have heard stories about "genital mutilation" but most people are not familiar with what the process entails.

The next story was from a woman who was about to go through that custom in a small Country in West Africa, but had to escape, hours before the beginning of the ceremony. She told me not to use her real name for the story, if I did write about it. Eno's parents were born in Togo, a small African nation on the West Coast of Africa. The conversation started when she saw the name on my chauffer license, she inquired if I am of African heritage, and I told her yes, she told me that she is as well.

She asked me if the custom of "genital mutilation" was practiced in the part of Africa where I was born. I told her it was a common custom in many parts of Africa, but it is a dying culture now, as many people do not practice it anymore. She said "Thank Heavens" it is dying away. She said she had a horrible experience, on her first trip to Togo. I asked her" what was the matter". By the way Eno was twenty-eight years old a few years ago, when she told me the following story.

When she was fifteen years old, her parents took her back to visit their Country. The plan was for her to stay for a few months before returning back to the United States. Her parents would be staying back in Togo; they decided to retire there. All things were set in place for the trip and Eno was very happy to be visiting her motherland. They soon set out on the trip. They traveled on Air France through Paris, and caught a connecting flight to Republic of Benin, and eventually reaching their town in Togo. Lots of family members were on hand to welcome them.

Everything was going on fine when they first arrived, and she was very happy to be back to the place she described as her "motherland". Relatives were coming in to see her in large numbers, and for her it was a very happy re-union because she was able to see all her relatives for the first time. This was her first trip to Togo, and she loved every bit of it. She soon joined her relatives in learning African dance. But somehow word got around in the village that she was not "circumcised" {Genital mutilation}. In places where this culture was practiced, it was called "circumcision" and sometimes women who were not circumcised were not courted for marriage.

So elders suggested to her parents that Eno could still perform the custom even at the age of fifteen. In those days, it was a shameful thing for families to have uncircumcised children, so many families would have their children circumcised so as to save the family the disgrace and shame of having an uncircumcised child. So Eno's parents accepted the idea but Eno was not informed of their decision.

A native doctor {local untrained doctor} was contacted, and arrangements were finalized about the day when Eno would undergo the process. Usually the operation involves the removal of the female clitoris; the procedure is performed without the use of anesthesia, through the use of crude and locally made instruments.

The date was settled, still Eno was not aware of the arrangements. But about four days to the day of the operation, Eno's parents called her into their bedroom and explained to her about the ceremony, re-assuring her of their love. Eno was not convinced because questions she asked them were not fully explained.

The following day word leaked out in the village, particularly among the kids who were making jokes about her, because she had not been circumcised. Eventually one of the girls asked Eno, if she was going to be circumcised, and Eno denied it, but she soon learnt what the operation was all about. She asked her parents about it, this time the parents told her the ceremony was called "circumcision", and it was necessary in other for her to be married when the time comes.

Eno promised her parents that the operation could only be performed to her dead body. She asked her parents what was the difference between the ceremony and genital mutilation; parents said that genital mutilation was just used by the West nations to put down the culture. Eno's mother assures her that she was also circumcised, and she is happy she did.

Meanwhile Eno began planning her escape without her parent's knowledge. One of her nieces came to her aid, and secretly arranged for her to escape to her house, without anybody knowing. Her niece was educated in France, so it was easier for her to understand her feelings about genital mutilation.

Their secret plot was for Eno to escape, the night before the ceremony to her niece's house, and then she would drive her to neighboring Republic of Benin from where she would be assisted back to the United States. So the plot was finalized and sealed.

The night before the ceremony, things were calm; Eno had her dinner with her parents, and went to bed a little earlier than usual. Meanwhile her parents thought that she had been convinced about undergoing the process. At about two o'clock in the morning, five hours before the ceremony, Eno got up from her bed, and quietly put together a few of her personal belongings, but in the process she heard some noise coming from her parents room. The noise Eno made had awakened her mom from sleep. Her mom decided to check out Eno's room to make sure she was okay.

When Eno saw the lights on the hall way lit, she quickly put her little bag under her bed and jumped back to her bed. The doorknob to her room was turned, and the door opened, it was her mum, but Eno was lying down on the bed, under the blanket pretending to be sound asleep. Her mother called her by her name, "Eno, Eno are you all right"?

Eno said nothing, and her mother thought that she was fast asleep, and left her room. Eno waited for another hour, meanwhile her niece was getting worried, because she was supposed to have made it to her place by then, but Eno was nowhere to be found. The time was then 3 am, and Eno got up again, she quietly opened the wooden window, and climbed out of the room, holding her little personal belongings with her.

She made it through one wall, but had to climb the fence to be totally out of the compound. She climbed the fence, but she fell back down, and the neighbor's dog barked at the noise. Eno was worried for a moment; she does not want the dog to awaken the neighbors or her parents up. She waited until the dog stopped barking to try again.

But she was determined, knowing that it was now or never, so she tried for the second time and this time she made it to the top of the fence. She quietly climbed down, still grabbing her little bag with her. She made it down the wall, and walked to her niece's house, a short distance away. Her niece was still waiting, when Eno knocked at the door. Eno was let into the house. She talked for a few minutes with her niece about the trip.

They immediately set out on the trip to Republic of Benin, a short distance away. Meanwhile it was daybreak and her parents got up from sleep. Preparations for the ceremony were about to begin. The native doctor who was to perform the operation had arrived by now, carrying with him the objects and local instruments he needed for the operation, including two sharp, double-edged knives, and palm oil and other local instruments. The native doctor requested a few shots of liquor; Enos's father served him. The native doctor took his position, and sharpened his two knives. Eno's mother went directly into Enos's room to awaken her, thinking at that time, that she was still sleeping. She opened the door, and the bed was empty, and silence was in the air. Eno was nowhere to be found.

She called the attention of her husband. They searched the room, and she was not in the room. A search soon ensued throughout the village, without any result. Meanwhile Eno was now in the Republic of Benin. It was a mystery, as the news spread throughout the village of her disappearance. Her parents were devastated, but they hoped that Eno would soon return. The circumcision ceremony was cancelled.

Eno was dropped off in The Republic of Benin, by her niece, who had since returned home. In fact her niece was also present, for the ceremony as well. No one knew what happened. From a relative's house in The Republic of Benin, Eno returned back to the United States through the help of several people. On arrival to the United States, she called to notify her parents that she was safe. Eno was grateful to her niece for her assistance. She was able to get the entire account of what unfolded after she left for the United States from her niece. Nobody has been able to figure out how she escaped from the house. It remained a mystery because Eno did not want to implicate her niece in any way, fearing reprisals against her.

Eno now lives in the United States, and is married with one child. She has re-united with her parents and has been back to see them in Togo since the incident. I was truly moved by the story and her bravery, and I promised her that I would tell her story in a book, she said okay, on condition that her real name was not used.

Chapter 23
A Trip To Roscoe's In Boys Town

He was a handsome young man in his early thirties, well dressed in a dark suit; he just flew into the Chicago O'Hare International airport, from San Francisco, on a business trip. He gently sat down in my taxi, requesting me to take him to the Marriott hotel in Oakbrook, Illinois, an affluent suburb of Chicago.

When I left the airport premises, he notified me that the trip would be continuing into Chicago, after he checked in at the hotel. It was a pretty good fare and I started to mentally figure out, how much the fare would be. Depending on traffic conditions, I roughly came up with about eighty dollars estimate.

"My name is Dave," he told me, and he asked for mine, I introduced myself also.

After we passed the first toll gate at Irving Park road, he asked me if I knew the Roscoe's bar on North Halstead Avenue in Chicago, I told him yes, that I take a lot of customers over there very often. Roscoe's is one of the many gay bars along Halstead Avenue, an area referred to as Boy's Town.

Soon afterwards, Dave asked me if I was married, I said yes, with children, as I momentarily remembered the popular TV comedy "Married with Children". The trip continued as I wondered why these question, and they were personal questions I thought.

The next question soon unfolded. "Have you met a gay person before"? Dave asked, I said yes I have, but in my mind, I was beginning to feel uncomfortable with that line of questions, and I came up with an idea to change the conversation. I decided to do the questioning for a change, so before he could ask me another follow-up question, I had one for him.

"Where do you live" I asked him? His answer was quick to follow, " San Francisco" he said. What line of work are you in? I quickly followed up. "I am a computer programmer", he said. "That is a lucrative career," I added. 'I am doing very well" Dave replied. Momentarily I was running short of questions, and I soon approached another tollgate. After we went through the second tollgate, before I could come up with another question, Dave initiated the next one, but we were a few minutes to his first destination at that point.

However he was able to throw in one more question, "have you tried gay sex before"? No! I told him in a fairly loud voice reminding him again of my marital status, and we soon pulled into the Marriott Hotel on Twenty-second Street in Oakbrook. It was a moment of relief as I parked my taxi and unloaded Dave's luggage from the trunk, while the doorman took them from me. Dave asked me to wait for him to check into the hotel.

I cleared the ramp and parked the taxi in a designated parking space while I waited for him, meanwhile the meter ticked away. Taximeters are configured to operate with time and distance, so the longer I waited for him, the more the fare would be. As I waited for Dave, I wondered if he would resume this line of questions or not upon his return.

I reasoned that the odds are in favor that the questions would continue, because his last question obviously, demanded a follow-up, but only time would answer that. Ten minutes after our arrival, the doorman came to tell me that Dave said he would take an additional time, because he is taking a shower. The doorman gave me a bottle of coke, compliments of Dave. Should I take the coke or not, I momentarily thought. I was fairly thirsty at the time.

I took the coke and thanked the doorman. Dave soon returned, and the trip resumed, he told me again his next destination, was Roscoe's. I thanked him for the soft drink he sent to me.

We continued on the second leg of the trip through the I- 88 Toll road, and the trip to the loop would continue onto I -294-toll road. The last leg would be on I- 290 into the loop, continuing on Lakeshore drive and exiting onto Belmont Avenue to Halstead Avenue. So I had my route mapped out mentally. Soon I would know if our previous conversation has been rested or not.

The answer was not far behind. "Do you have any animosity against gay people"? Dave quickly asked me. In my mind I said oh no not again. I assured Dave that I have no animosity against anyone, and that I have a few gay friends. "Do you want to try gay sex"? He asked me again. I said No Dave, but thank you for asking, that I have no desire for that lifestyle. "But you said you have some gay friends" he followed up. I do, I replied, but it is a casual friendship. As we approached the entrance to I 290, there was traffic back up, the notorious "Hillside Strangler traffic" was working against me, but I quickly remembered that longer time in traffic also translates into a bigger fare, and this thought soon became a consolation for all the time we spent in traffic.

My feeling at this point regarding Dave was that of bewilderment. I was not particularly happy about the obvious advance, which at that time had become apparent, but at the same time I was not very upset either, for one thing, the thought that he found me attractive, was very flattery. To find myself on the receiving end of such a proposal is something that continued to bewilder, and pleasantly surprise me as well.

But at this time Dave's intentions had been expressed, and it was clear to me where he was going. Despite my negative responses, Dave's attempted courtship did not stop there. "Would you like to have a drink with me at the bar"? He further asked me. No, but thanks anyway. I reminded him that I was on duty, and could not drink and drive because it would endanger my life and that of my passengers.

I would rather have an increased tip was the thought that revolved on my mind, if he wants to show an appreciation for my services to him. As soon as we cleared the "Hillside Strangler traffic", the rest of the trip into the loop was quick, and Dave may have asked the last of his questions, I imagined. His consolation would come when he arrives at the Roscoe's. There are hundreds of gay persons and I thought that, with his gentle personality and good looks, he would meet someone without any problems.

As we passed the loop along the Lakeshore drive, Dave took notice of the beautiful skyline, and a great panoramic view of the Chicago shoreline. The City is beautiful Dave said. This was a relief and an assurance to me that the conversation had shifted. I welcomed that remark and for the rest of the trip I gave him a mini description of tourist attractions along the city shoreline. I pointed out the Museum Campus, the Buckingham fountain, the Grant Park, the Navy Pier, and the Lincoln Park Zoo, as well as the Belmont harbor.

A panoramic view of Chicago skyline, with the United Center at the background

We exited into Belmont Avenue, and three minutes later we arrived at Roscoe's in Boys town. The fare was about seventy-eight dollars; Dave passed up to me a one hundred dollar bill and asked me to keep the change. I thanked him for his kindness, wishing him well, as admirers for this handsome gentleman, were peeping through the glass windows of Roscoe's. I wondered if my answers to him were rude in any way. No, another voice re-assured me. He left the taxi and walked into the bar, and disappeared among the jubilant Roscoe's crowd.

Chapter 24
Summertime Stories

Summertime in Chicago is simply fun. After the harsh winter months, summer rolls in with a type of "irrational exuberance" if I may borrow from Alan Greenspan. Chicago residents are happy after the winter hibernation, and it is time for women to get rid of the layers of winter clothing and show the beauty of their legs, and upper chest. {For those that have one}

But Chicago has some of the most beautiful women, beauty is however in the eye of the holder, but if you have been to Chicago, I am sure you would agree with me, that the statement is not an overstatement. During the summer months, Chicago's women are not shy to show their body. Part of the reason is the enduring heat and humidity, which transforms this winter wonderland into a tropical paradise during the few summer months. Chicago's weather is quite unique one day is warm, and the next day is cool, this is part of what makes this city interesting.

Chicago residents love their seasons; there is a popular saying in Chicago that "if you don't like the current weather, wait for another hour". Summer is my favorite season in Chicago. Every now and then during the winter, I pick up some passengers who tells me, that they love cold weather and snow. My simple suggestion to those passengers is to move to Alaska or Siberia. Summer is a glorious time in Chicago. The city is bustling with all kinds of activity. The Grant Park is the venue for all kinds of festivals. The lakefront is full of both tourists and native Chicagoans. Many joggers, skaters, cyclists, are all competing for space on the narrow tracks stretching for many miles on the lakefront.

One of the retractable bridges raised across the Chicago River, allowing boats to cross the waterway

All kinds of boats are streaming in and out of the Chicago River, through the many raised bridges into Lake Michigan. The sailboats may pass as many as nine or ten of such bridges, before entering the harbor. Chicago, not Venice has the highest number of drawbridges than any other city in the world, a little bit of history here. When the bridges are raised, they further disrupt the traffic in the loop, which is particularly hectic during the summer, due in part to construction activities, and road closures.

Colorful Sail boats on Lake Michigan, a typical Summer sight in the Windy City.

Many Sailboats are seen on the horizon, on the lake, glowing with as assortment of colors. Cruise ships are sailing in and out of the Navy Pier Harbor; my favorite is the“Spirit of Chicago”. If you visit Chicago during the summer, make sure you take a cruise down the Chicago River. You’ll get a lot of history about Chicago and its wonderful architectures. Traffic on Lakeshore drive is often bumper-to-bumper, part of the reason being that so many festivals take place in the Grant Park. The most popular is the “Taste of Chicago” offering ethnic cuisine from basically every corner of the world.

More Sail boats on Chicago's waterfront, with John Hancock building towering above other buildings

On a particular "Taste of Chicago" weekend, I was heading to the Navy Pier, to drop off some passengers, because the traffic caused by the "Taste of Chicago" was so bad, I decided to exit on Randolph Street, and use Illinois street. When I got to the stoplight at the intersection of Illinois Street and lower lakeshore drive, I took notice of a group of pretty women walking across the lower lakeshore drive.

The popular annual "Taste of Chicago" festival draw millions to the Grant Park

One lady among the group attracted more attention than others. It was a long line of pedestrians crossing the street, all heading to the Navy Pier. The traffic Police was in no hurry to let us through. As this lady walked closer to my taxi, I noticed why she was causing such an uproar- she had a see- through mini dress that revealed her entire feminine characteristics.

Next to her was another young lady with a split dress. Chicago women love split dresses, and I am sure that men admirers like them as well. But the problem with the woman wearing the split dress, in this instance was that the split on her dress was a little longer than most others, the dress was split in front, and on her back

The lakefront was a little breezy that day, so the young lady had a little problem to deal with. The wind was blowing her split dress in all directions revealing her underwear. She was busy trying to hold her dress down in position, but the wind did not permit her to do that. Even the traffic Policeman took notice, and was momentarily distracted from his work, making the motorists wait for a longer time, before passing them.

But the cop finally signaled us to move on, and I turned into Illinois street leading to Navy Pier. At the Navy Pier, I dropped off my passengers, and since it was time for the weekly fireworks, I decided to park my taxi, and watch the fireworks. It was a good break for me as well.

The sky was lit with an assortment of fire works, as another glorious summer night soon gave way to Chicago nightlife, as Rush Street comes alive, its party time in the windy city. Summertime in the Chicago is fun, and Rush Street is the heart of nightlife in the windy city.

Rush Street, the center of Night life in Chicago

Chapter 25
Political Dialogues

He told me he was in his early seventies, when our conversations began. I generally avoid political conversations but in this case, it was unavoidable. My passenger very badly wanted the argument. He introduced himself as James, a veteran of World War II, he informed me. He also told me he took part in the Normandy invasion. I had no way of judging if James was telling me the truth or not, because I asked him specific questions on the Normandy battle, and his answers were very vague. My instinct tells me he was exaggerating, but if he took part in the liberation of France, he deserves a lot of thanks.

I picked him up at Franklin and Adams Streets, near the Sears Tower. As soon as he made an entry into my taxi, he handed me a written instruction. The directions were to take the Kennedy {I-90} to Pulaski Avenue to Montrose Avenue and turn right on Montrose.

The Kennedy was bumper to bumper, but at his request I crawled along with the rest of the traffic. His first question to me was one of those questions that cab drivers generally dislike, because of the way such questions are framed. James was very controversial, as well as confrontational. It became obvious to me that he was looking for a debate, so I decided to give him one.

You are not from here are you? He asked me. Cab drivers generally prefer to avoid such questions, simply because it re-enforces the society's perceptions about their alien status. But if you want to ask a question in that direction, a more "politically correct" question would be, where were you born?

But I was not going to ignore James' question so I told him that I was born in Africa. He then asked me, "Where the hell is that cannibal called Bukavuvu"? For some reason I don't like people asking me questions using this particularly format. I replied him, "who the hell is he"? "You know that African brutal dictator who ate human beings, he said". I reminded him that there are several brutal dictators in Africa, and none of them was called Bukavuvu. Are you sure you pronounced his name correctly? I asked him.

James said the dictator once ruled Central African Republic, oh I said you meant Bokassa. He said "yes". I informed him that Bokassa died in 1996, and reminded him that Bokassa was once a captain in the French army. "What about Idi Amin", James asked me next. I told him that I was not sure, that he might be living in one of the North

African Countries, or Saudi Arabia. Both men were evil men I told James, but their crimes were not worse than those of Adolph Hitler, or Mussolini.

He moved over to environmental problems facing the African continent, raising the issue of the plight of elephants, lions, and other endangered species in Africa. He also talked about the deforestation problems going on in Africa, as well as in South America. He made a particular reference to Ivory Coast and the rain forest of Brazil. I assured him that I agreed with him over those concerns, that humans are gradually destroying the planet.

But I told him that while he singled out the developing nations in Africa and South America, as contributing to those problems, he did not blame the industrialized world for the worsening industrial pollution, as well as the destruction of the ozone layer. Did you read Gore's book, "Earth in a balance"? I asked him. He said those democrats are part of the problem, that he does not trust them either.

He asked how I knew all that, and still driving cab, I asked him, if he was implying that cab drivers are ignorant, James said most of the ones he knew were ignorant. I told James that his biases are coming out the more we discuss, noting that he blamed African and South

America countries, thinks Cab drivers are illiterates, dislikes democrats, who else do you dislike? I asked him.

My purpose here, I told him was not to defend anyone, and I agreed with him that many African leaders are selfish and corrupt, but he failed to present a balanced argument about the environmental destruction problem, by not pointing out the problem of pollution by the G7 and now G8 Countries who account for over sixty percent of the global industrial pollution.

I decided to put him on the defensive, by asking him what trade he was involved with, he said "Diamond business", telling me that he was previously based in Israel and used to travel to South Africa buying diamonds. I said ah ha! You were one of the supporters of the Apartheid South African Government, by trading with them during those days, and you are now lecturing me about the problems in Africa. He kept quiet momentarily. I realized that I had just scored a knockout punch with that statement because James had no answer or rebuttal for that.

Soon we approached the exit he specified, and he was becoming uncomfortable for the conversation, as he sought for an exit strategy. But I also knew that we would be getting to his destination soon. The argument was so heated that I did not know that at one point during the debate, James pulled off his dentures, and put it in a clear plastic bag.

We soon pulled up to his destination; he horridly exited from the taxi after paying for the fare. I knew it was a hot exchange, he did not give me any tips, and I was not looking for one. I said bye and drove off, one block later I looked at the back of the taxi. As a rule, I always check to make sure that the last passenger did not forget any of their personal belongings, and guess what I found. James forgot his dentures inside the taxi.

I had some kick out of that. So I quickly turned around, and drove back to the location where I dropped him, and luckily James was already looking for it. I pulled up and asked him if he forgot something in the taxi. He started laughing as he opened the back door, and grabbed his dentures. He told me that I have changed his view that all cab drivers are dumb, I told him it was not my intended objective, that I simply arm myself with facts. On his dentures which he forgot inside my taxi, I said to him, “don’t worry I truly understand how it happened”, James continued to laugh as I made my departure.

Chapter 26
Conversations With Mohammed

Taxi -conversations often involves political issues. Venue for my next story was the O'Hare staging area at the airport. As indicated earlier waiting time for fares from the airport is often long. September 11 is a date that would go down in the annals of history as the turning point of another chapter in the ways nations relate with one another. On that eventful day, I just dropped off a fare at the Sears Tower in the loop.

The magnificent Sears Tower was for a long time the tallest building in the world

People were streaming out of the Sears Tower building in what looked like a systematic and orderly evacuation. At that point I knew immediately that something was wrong, but I was not sure what the problem at that point was. I tuned on the WBBM station, a twenty-four-hour news radio station where I get news about all the current happenings.

I soon realized that the World Trade Center in New York City had been attacked. It was dreaded news in fact. In the days and weeks following this tragic event there were all kinds of debates and conversations about the tragedy and implications for us all. At this time, I no longer drive taxi fulltime, but sometimes I would lease a taxi to supplement my income. I particularly remember an advice given to me by another author, who is also a friend of mine. He told me that writing and publishing is a tough business particularly for new authors. In that regard, he advised me to keep a part time job until such a time that my writing career is well established. So I continued to moonlight with taxi-driving on a part-time basis.

My most challenging and emotional debate took place at the O'Hare Staging area between a fellow cab driver and myself. He told me that he was born in Egypt, and called himself Mohammed. No surprises there because, I jokingly told him, I have never met a Moslem person whose first, middle or last name did not include Mohammed. He laughed.

Two weeks after the start of the U.S. led battle against the Taliban and the Al Quida Network of Osama Bin Laden, I was at the airport waiting in my taxi for a fare. Mohammed walked up to me and asked for my views about what happened in New York. "It was a barbaric act by evil men, " I told him. We sat down inside my taxi where the following heated debate took place.

"What is your name?" he asked. My name is Paul I told him.

"Are you a Moslem"? He asked

"Do Moslems answer Paul"? I inquired from him. He laughs.

"Why are you a Christian"? He asked me. "Because of the peace of mind" I told him.

"Come on Paul, Islam is a more peaceful religion," he said. "You are right Mohammed, and Osama just proved it by killing thousands of innocent people including Christians, Moslems, Jews and Gentiles, men, women and children"

This was like throwing a bomb when I made that statement. "Osama is a good man, by standing up to the United States"

Mohammed said. “What about the Palestinian people being slaughtered by Israel,” he further charged.” Look I am against that as well,” I told him.” But the U.S. supports Israeli atrocities against the Palestinian people” Mohammed charged.” Can we take these issues one at a time Mohammed” I suggested.

Please do not misunderstand me I told him. I have some problems with some U.S. foreign policy. When similar Moslem groups massacred the Ibos in Northern Nigeria, the world did not act to save the unfolding genocide. But please understand that the U.S. is a Country acting for the interest of U.S. citizens. The problem between Israel and the Palestinians would be resolved through a negotiated peace settlement. “So long as the U.S. is behind Israel, the problem would never be solved,” Mohammed argues. He contends that the Intifada by the Palestinians would continue indefinitely. “Look Mohammed, the Palestinians have made their point through the Intifada”. “It is becoming counter productive now because Israel is a much stronger opponenent,” I said. “Unfortunately the innocent Palestinians and Israelis are being slaughtered in the process, in an unending cycle of violence”. I further pointed out.

Mohammed argued that Israel does not have the right to occupy Palestinian land. "I think you are mixing apples and oranges," I said. I am not here to defend the Israelis. My point is that the Israeli-Palestinian dispute would be resolve through a compromise between both parties. If anyone in Palestine is thinking that Israel would vanish from the face of the earth, it is simply an illusion, I added.

Mohammed said the whole Israeli-Palestinian dispute is not fair. Life is not always fair I informed him. His point is that there is no basis for negotiations between the Israelis and the Palestinians because Israel is the aggressor by occupying the Palestinian lands. I reminded him however that the basis of negotiations is for settlement.

Naturally, if someone takes your property, if you can force them to relinquish it, do so. But in this case it is obvious that the Palestinians do not have the military know-how to force Israel to relinquish their property-a negotiated settlement is their only choice.

"Well that's why the world needs Osama," Mohammed points out.

"I totally disagree with you, as far as I am concerned, Osama is a mass murderer," I added."He is also an opportunist, trying to instigate a Jihad against the Christians"

"What about the Crusaders"? Mohammed asked me

"I am not happy with that movement, but as far as I know, there are no modern crusaders in the year 2001, the crusades took place a long time ago"

"Osama is also right by trying to remove the U.S. from occupying Arab lands" Mohammed pointed out.

"As far as I know, the U.S. was invited by Saudi Arabia when Iraq invaded Kuwait" I replied him.

"The Saudis are American Puppets; the United States is exploiting Arab oil" Mohammed countered, "Doesn't the U.S. pay for those oil"? I asked Mohammed.

"Look what the U.S. does better than the rest of the world is technological innovation,"I further said.

"What's that"? Mohammed asked.

"Research and production capabilities" I answered him.

"You sound educated, why are you driving a cab"? Mohammed asked me.

"Do you mean that educated people don't drive cab"? I asked.

I explained to Mohammed that what I am saying is simply a common sense thing. Third world countries should understand that the reason why the U.S. is the leading world economy comes from years of hard work and stable political climate. I don't mean that everything the U.S. did along the way is right, for instance the slave trade would always remain in the dark pages of the U.S. history.

"How can Third Word countries compete with the U.S."? Mohammed asked.

The only way to do that is through investments in technological education, and the eradication of bribery and corruption, which is an impediment against progress, in most developing nations.

"The U.S. is corrupt too," Mohammed charges.

"There is corruption everywhere but of a lesser magnitude in the U.S. compared with third world countries". "At least there is accountability in the U.S; a process of checks and balances between the three branches of government, these qualities are lacking in third world countries" I pointed out to him.

Mohammed contends that the U.S. helps to keep third world nations poor. I don't think this is an objective of the U.S. government. I reminded him. This is simply the consequence of the imbalance in the global production and distribution of goods and services.

"What about Saudi Arabia, Why are they not as rich and progressive as the U.S."? Mohammed asked me.

Well they are not, because the royal families are keeping all the oil revenues to themselves; again this goes to illustrate the bribery and corruption point that I raised earlier, You have only two classes in Saudi Arabia-the rich and the poor.

The other problem I pointed out to Mohammed is the lack of separation of church and state in Saudi Arabia. Mohammed hastily points out that Islam has strict codes that regulate people, which is important for governing as well.

"I have a question for you Mohammed," I said.

"What question he asked"?

Please tell me any country in the world where Shari a {Islamic based government} system has worked, from Saudi Arabia, to Iran, from Sudan to Afghanistan. I asked.

Mohammed said that it works in Saudi Arabia. "Give me a break," I answered him. With all the human rights violations common in Saudi Arabia, you consider that nation as a good example of a successful Shari a government? I asked him. Until the Taliban emerged in Afghanistan, Saudi Arabia was one of the leading repressive governments in the world.

"Tell me Mohammed, you said you are from Egypt"?

"Yes" he said.

"You are condemning the U.S. right, do you know how much foreign aid, the U.S. gives to your country in one year"? "About two billion dollars a year" He said.

Well you are right, and you are condemning the United States? I asked.

"If you don't like the U.S. why are you living and working here? I asked him.

"I just came here to drive taxi," he said.

"You mean that there are no taxis in Cairo"? "What about you, can't you drive in Nigeria"? Mohammed asked me. "Well I recognize that the U.S. has many more opportunities, and that's why I came here", to improve my chances.

"I am leaving, Paul, I enjoyed the conversation" Mohammed told me. "No you did not", I replied, Mohammed laughs.

"I enjoyed it as well, hopefully you have heard the truth today" I told him. Mohammed laughed, telling me that I have heard the truth as well and soon his taxi line was signaled down to the terminal for a pick-up, as the conversation ended.

Chapter 27
Conversations With Kathy

One cold December evening, a new year's eve, in Chicago on the corner of Belmont and Broadway, a passenger stood there waiting for a taxi. I did not know why this particular passenger hailed my taxi. Two other empty cabs were ahead of mine. They were not stopped. As soon as I neared the corner where this passenger stood, she signaled me to stop. I did. At that time I was driving for American United.

The Author in his American United Taxi finds time to feed pigeons when conditions are too hectic

She had army pants, a matching baseball cap facing backwards. Her camouflage army pants were neatly inserted into black army boot. She walked like a soldier. She took a few steps and grabbed and opened the right rear door of the taxi and landed on the back seat with some force.

"Please take me to the corner of Division and Laramie" she told me.

"Okay" I replied, and turned the meter on. "I waited for an American United Taxi because they are the only taxi company we find in our neighborhood," she told me.

"How do you do" she inquired " I am fine"

"My name is Kathy" "Paul is mine," I told her.

Kathy asked me to take Lakeshore drive down to the Eisenhower, and exit on Laramie.

"Are you sure it's the way you want", I explained to her that her preferred route is about two miles off course.

"That's fine, I just want to take the express" We jumped into southbound lakeshore drive.

"How is your day"? She asked again "Its okay" I told her.

"What about yours"? I asked Kathy, not as good, she said.

"What's the matter I inquired"?

"My life is full of problems right now" Kathy said, I told her that I was sorry to hear that, but wished her well.

"Do you want to hear my story", Kathy asked me.

"Yes" I told her. Here is the rest of her story. Kathy was pregnant at the age of seventeen, and her first child was born seven weeks prematurely. Her son spent many weeks in the incubator at the hospital. Not only did her child inherit some medical conditions at birth, he was also born with cocaine in his system. Kathy used cocaine during the pregnancy.

How could a teenager, her age afford an expensive drug as cocaine you may ask? The answer is simple. Kathy did not have to buy cocaine. She did not even have to leave her house to get cocaine either. All she needed to do was walk down to the basement of the house where she lived, and open a small safe buried underground. She has all the cocaine in the world at her fingertips. Her boyfriend was a drug pusher on the Westside. He was twenty at the time. His drug trade was going on fine at the time. They both planned to get married one day. At nineteen, Kathy was pregnant again with her second son. Like her first son, he was also born with cocaine in his system.

Before Kathy delivered her second child, undercover agents busted her fiancée. He was tried with possession of illegal drugs with intent to distribute, and was convicted and sentenced to twelve years in the federal penitentiary.

This was devastation for Kathy as she began using drugs more heavily. Both of her two boys were eventually taken away from her. They now live together in a foster home, but Kathy was granted a supervised visitation rights. As Kathy's drug problem grew, she met another woman who promised to help her.

Kathy moved in with her, soon intimate relations developed between them, and Kathy's lifestyle changed - she became a Lesbian. Her problem she said with tears dripping out of her eyes, she loves her two boys, and would like to get them back one day.

On her last visit with her boys, she went in the company of her lover, who bought some toys for them. Kathy is worried that her lover may soon abandon her because of her heavy drug problem, but she told me that she would be going to a drug treatment center in a few weeks time. Kathy's boys are coming of age, and have started to ask Kathy whom her lover is, because she buys them many gifts. Kathy said she has not always been a lesbian. From time to time, she engages in heterosexual sex. Part of her reason for turning to lesbian lifestyle was because of necessity. She hopes to get married to a man one day but according to her most of the young men she grew up with in their neighborhood are either in prison or killed in gang fighting. It is truly a war zone in the neighborhood where she grew up, she told me.

I was moved by her story. Here is a real case of a dysfunctional family. Basically every person in the story is a victim. From two children in a foster home born with cocaine in their system, to the young father locked away in prison. Kathy is a drug addict and her lover is a victim of Kathy's circumstance. We soon pulled into her destination and her lover was waiting for her. Her lover paid me for the fare. She kissed Kathy. They held hands, hugged and disappeared into the house.

Chapter 28
Halloween Tales

Some passengers would simply talk you to death. Have you been in a conversation with people who simply do not brake when they talk? You know it is a problem. It is also frustrating because you don't want to appear rude when you are in a two-way conversation. Communication is simply a two way street. That's why we have a word called "dialogue". But if people want to engage in a "monologue" that is also their prerogative as well, but they should engage in monologues when no one is around them.

The story here is about a passenger, picked up at 3300 block of inner Lakeshore drive on a Halloween morning. He is obviously a gambler, because he was heading to the Off-track Betting Facility on Weed Street. "Hello how are you," he inquired from me. As I was about to say fine, he started talking about the beautiful whether Chicago was enjoying that particular morning.

"I am from New York," he said further. For the next few minutes, he compared Chicago and New York City. Well all I could add is "Yeah" I managed to squeeze that in only at the very second he is gasping for air. "I was a cab driver in New York for ten years" he continued. I said "yeah, they ran you out of New York City"? "No" he said, explaining further that he was tired of taking insult from passengers. Well I understand, I am receiving one right now I thought to myself.

"How much does a Medallion cost in Chicago now"? He asked. In New York it costs about two hundred thousand dollars, he added. I never did get a chance to tell him how much it costs in Chicago, when he abruptly changed the topic again, and I was ready to dump him then. "Do you like my hair style"? For the first time he waited for an answer. "For a Halloween day, yes" I told him. He had one of those "punk style" hairdos, which I did not like anyway. He gave me a history of the hairdo for a few minutes. Thank God I just pulled up to the address he gave me.

I asked him to pay the fare, but he was more interested in another conversation, but the meter was quickly ticking away. "Can you stop the meter now" he asked, Sir you have the option to pay now, but if you still want more conversation, I will leave the meter on until you pay for the fare. He decided to pay me off at that point, no tip of course, but I was happy the trip was over. Many cabbies would tell you that such passengers don't generally tip much anyway. What a relief, I went straight to the nearest coffee shop for a break.

Chapter 29
Halloween Robbery

Spooky things happen on Halloween nights in Chicago, but not in my wildest dream would I imagine being attacked in this manner. It was an incident on the corner of Orleans and Oak streets, a few blocks from the notorious Cabrini Green apartments. It was about 7pm on a Halloween evening and I was returning to the loop from a drop off in Buck town. A red light on the corner of Oak and Orleans had just turned red. As I waited for the green light, suddenly three objects landed on my right front door. At first I thought I was being stoned, but I did not do anything that could trigger that. Before the light turned green, three more objects hit the side glass on the window. I hurriedly drove through the red light, fearing for my life.

The most famous of Chicago's Housing projects, Cabrini Green

I drove to the Shell Station on the corner of Orleans and Chicago Avenue to inspect the damage. It was raw eggs that landed on the taxi, half a dozen of them. It was not a big deal, only a few minutes of clean up time, requiring a scrubbing car wash. The thought that came to my mind was how could these youngsters spend their money to buy eggs and waste them this way. Well, I don't blame them because they were lucky to be born in America the land of plenty. The half dozen eggs they wasted at my car were enough for a family breakfast. It was very messy though, so I was about to go to the car wash for a clean up, wondering if I should report the incident to the cops.

I decided to report the incident to the Chicago police hoping they would chase the teenagers from that area. I flagged down a squad car to relay the incident to the officers. “What is the matter”? Officer A asked me.

“I was attacked” I replied.

“What do you mean?” Officer B asked.

“A group of young Cabrini boys hauled eggs on my taxi” I told them.

The Officers laughed, “What’s funny?” I asked.

“Well you are lucky” Officer B replied.

“You mean I was lucky teenagers attacked me with raw eggs”

“You should be happy it was not bullets that hit your taxi” officer A said to me.

“The best advice for you is to go and have a good car wash,” Officer B said.

After the car wash, I went back to work and soon picked up a young passenger who told me he was going to a Halloween party. His face was painted with several colors. His face looked more like a cat. I did not at the time suspect any thing unusual after all he was young, and it was Halloween. My young passenger asked me to take him to

Division and California neighborhood, telling me he was running late for the Halloween party.

As soon as we passed the corner of Western and Division he asked me to turn right on one of the side streets.

By now it was about 10pm and getting a little late for working in unfamiliar neighborhoods. It was the Puerto Rican neighborhoods many cabbies avoid such areas. As I approached a poorly lit segment of the street my cat-faced passenger asked me to pull over. I stopped. I looked behind to tell him how much the fare was and a small gun was pointed at me. It looked like a 22 -caliber pistol, but I was not sure because I only had a few seconds glimpse of the weapon. He said, "Don't do any thing stupid, just give me your wallet, and do it quick" I said "okay", and reached for my wallet and handed it over to him.

He jumped into a nearby alley and fled leaving the taxi door open. I managed to move the taxi a few yards away from the alley before getting out to close the back door, fearing my attacker may strike me. I accelerated immediately and left the vicinity. As soon as I entered Division Street, I pulled into a nearby gas station to reflect on what just happened. I looked behind the back seat and realized that he left the gun at the back seat. I walked around and picked up the weapon; it was a toy gun. I felt an increased adrenaline flow, that this teenager was able to pull a robbery with a toy gun. He fooled me. Well I did the right thing anyway. It is always good to play it safe.

I only lost twenty-five dollars in the robbery. I kept two wallets. One was packed with one-dollar bills totaling twenty-five dollars, I usually keep two wallets, and one of the wallets was the one I gave to the robber. That strategy worked because the twenty dollar single notes made the wallet thick, creating the impression that it was packed with a lot of money. The second wallet still with me contained the rest of my money. Should I report it to the police again I contemplated. No, after all the police ridiculed me, when I reported the incident at Cabrini Green, where I was attacked with raw eggs.

This time, who knows what fun they would make of me. This incident lends itself to such a ridicule I reasoned. I tossed the toy gun into a trashcan and pulled away. I have had enough for the day, as I went straight to my home. It was a crazy Halloween night indeed.

Chapter 30
Sex for Money

It was about 11.30 pm on a Friday night, I just returned from a late night airport run. After my passenger was dropped off at the Embassy Suites on State and Ohio, I drove to a nearby Excalibur nightclub on Ontario and Dearborn to wait for my next fare. I was the third taxi on the line, as we patiently waited for fares.

Two young men walked up to me, they asked me if I could do them a favor. 'What favor"? I asked. The younger of the two guys said, "Where can we get some Ganja" "say what" I replied. "Can you tell us where we can find some Ganja?" the older guy said. I was a little naive, and did not know what Ganja was at that time.

Well thinking they meant girls; I told them to try the Excalibur club behind them. "Do you know what Ganja is?" they asked me, informing me it was "grass", or "marijuana" "Excuse me" I replied. Sorry gentlemen I don't know where you can find that.

They walked away from me and a street hawker approached them momentarily. They talked for a few minutes, and walked away towards LaSalle Street. Ganja I later found out was a Jamaican word for Marijuana. We all learn one day at a time.

A few moments after that, I moved on to the number one position. An unusual passenger approached my cab from the direction of the Hard Rock Café. She had a very short sexy dress with high-heeled shoes. She walked like the night girls I thought. Her dress, handbag, and shoe were perfect matches. Her make- up was very loud. Her upper chest was half revealed to the point that you can almost see her protruding nipples. She quietly sat down in my taxi and asked me to take her to North Avenue and Kingsbury. Ah ha! it was the clue I noted, it was a hang out destination for night working girls.

We took off, as I turned the meter on. Three blocks away, her cell phone rang. She talked for a few minutes, details of the conversation I did not hear, but when she told me that she is changing her destination, it led me to believe that somebody, possibly a customer had just called her. "What's your new destination"? I asked.

"Please take me to Clybourn and Wrightwood area". I continued driving up on Clybourn Street as she directed.

A few turns from Wrightwood Avenue, she directed me to pull over in front of an apartment building. She did not know the exact apartment where her caller resided. So we waited for a few minutes. Soon a man emerged from the building. He entered the taxi. From the conversations going on, it was apparent that they did not know one another.

I wondered how the customer got her number, since they did not know themselves before. I quickly remembered that often working girls would pass out their business cards to prospective customers. In fact I have been given business cards by some working girls, who promised me that, if I referred some customers to them, they would give me twenty dollars for each reference. I usually toss their cards into the trashcan once I dropped them off. What do they think of me, am I a pimp or what? Any way, my passengers asked me to take them to Quality Inn on Halstead Avenue.

I turned the taxi around and headed back to the loop. Soon negotiations started. She told him she charges two hundred dollars an hour. They negotiated down to one hundred dollars an hour. They agreed to spend one hour together, and he would pay her hundred dollars and also pay the total taxi cost, in addition to the hotel room.

The male customer complained that, before this is all done, he would end up spending a fortune. In my mind I said why are you whining, after all, you made the decision and should know that love does not come cheap. We soon pulled into Quality Inn. He went in to pay for the room. Few minutes later, he emerged from the hotel. "No luck" he said. The hotel was sold out.

Damn! the lady said; where is our next destination? I asked. Try the motel six on Ontario. I was certain, that he wouldn't find a room there either, because it is one of the few budget motels in the loop, it sells out faster than other hotels. But any way I headed that way.

Soon she complained that she was loosing too much time, informing him, that he was going to pay her at the expiration of one hour, whether he secured a room or not. He insisted that no show, no money. A stalemate was beginning to unfold, and I started wondering about being paid for my services.

My worst fears were soon confirmed as Motel Six was also sold out. The male customer was now seeking for an exit strategy. The cab fare had reached twenty-five dollars by now. The lady was getting increasingly frustrated. He decided to try the Holiday Inn City Center. How this drama was going to end became my immediate concern. When the male customer asked me to go to the Holiday Inn City Center, it was apparent to me that he was about to bail out. Cab drivers learn quick lessons, and they don't take any more chances once they have been taken for a ride.

My lesson from that Hotel was learnt few months ago. I took a passenger to that hotel, and he asked me to wait for him so he can check if they had any rooms. He asked me to leave the meter running because if the hotel is sold out, he would need me to take him to another hotel. I said okay. He went into the hotel and never came out. I waited for fifteen minutes, and he was nowhere to be found.

So I went into the hotel to look for him. I asked the registration clerk if my passenger had checked into the hotel. They informed me that he walked in and asked if they had rooms. They told him that the hotel was sold out, and then he walked away through the Fairbanks side- door. It was then that I realized that my passenger had fooled me. While I waited for him at the front door; he left the hotel through the side-door.

This scenario was still vivid on my mind when this male customer asked me to take them to that hotel. It will not happen again I promised myself. When I pulled to the Holiday Inn, I demanded that he should pay me for the fare so far. He said he will pay me on his return, I refused, and he saw the look on my face and decided that I was pretty serious about that, so he paid me the total fare at that time.

Meanwhile the lady's frustration was building. He walked into the hotel after paying me, as we sat waiting for him. Since I have been paid, I decided that I would not get into this drama. Ten minutes passed, he was not yet back. The lady asked me to go and see what he was doing. I suggested that she should go instead. She did, and came back with a rage. "He left the hotel through the back door" she screamed.

"I am going to call the police on him" she added. "What would be his charge if the police found him"? I asked her. "He did pay me for the fare" I added. She looked at me and said, "You know you have a point". She walked out of the taxi full of rage.

As I reflected on this incident, I concluded that there was no crime, nor victim. I was paid for the fare, the woman did not give up anything, and the guy spent some money and got nothing in return. What a night indeed it was.

Section III

Taxi Humor Stories

Chapter 31
Bachelorette Story

Bachelorette nights are indeed quite memorable in Chicago Often on Saturday nights one can see groups of young girls wandering from bar to bar celebrating the last days of a soon to be married bride. The groups range from five to as many as eight. One of the members of such group is usually the aspiring bride. She is always distinguishable from the rest of the group from her dressing.

Usually the girls are for the most part drunk, they are very rowdy and wild. They are "bar hopping", simply wandering from one bar to the next. Rush Street is usually the center of such celebrations. It was a Saturday evening, on the corner of State Street and Division, the heart of nightlife activity in the loop.

I was just coming out of the Dunkin Donoughts shop on the corner of Clerk and Division from a fifteen-minute coffee break. I saw a group of about six girls celebrating a bachelorette night. They were in a very jubilant mood and quite hyped up. Two of the girls had a special "penis shaped drinking cup", with drinking straws inserted in them.

One of the girls was drinking from the cup as they walked to the cheers of young passers by, mostly young men in their early twenties. A sudden scene soon unfolded. The bachelorette gang had just captured two young men passing by them. They circled around the men.

They two men were obviously strangers, and did not know the girls before. Some negotiations soon began and I was very curious to find out what was going on. So I walked closer, to have a better view of what was going on. The boys had no chances of escaping from the girls because the girls were quite determined to achieve their objective. What is the objective of the girls, I wondered. I soon learnt the details of the negotiations.

The girls were pressuring the boys to expose their penis to their view. At first it seemed that the boys were objecting to that request, and were not going to yield. But the girls were not about to let them go either. I was determined to see the resolution of this drama so I hanged around.

The matter would be resolved one way or the other. The girls can give up and let the two young men go, or stand their ground. On the other hand, the men could force their way through, but they did not want to do that, they also had the option of entertaining the bachelorette gang. The decision was soon taken.

One of the boys decided to yield to the girl's request. To the cheers of the girls, he pulled down his pants and underwear, exposing his butts and penis. The girls roared and cheered at that. The exposure lasted for a few seconds. Every one was satisfied. The men were released from the inner circle where they were. They walked away in one direction and the bachelorette gang moved on in the opposite direction. My coffee break was finally over as well. Dramas like that happen all the time in this wonderful city.

Dentist Phobia Story

. Are you among those with fear of "Root Canals"? If so, this story will re-assure you that you are not alone. This story was given to me by one of my passengers from Dallas. It was her experience on her last trip to a Dentist. Lila as she introduced herself was experiencing toothache at nights, often disrupting her night sleep. On the insistence of her husband, Lila decided to visit the Dentist to have her teeth checked up.

On this particular night, the pain was so intense that she had no sleep at all. Early in the morning she looked up the yellow pages for information on local area Dentists. She chose a particularly Dentist fairly close to her home. The name of the Dentist looked like Korean, Taiwanese, or Chinese she told me, you know such names that have three alphabets she explained to me.

It was 9am in the morning, and Lila took off for the Dentist Office. By now the pain was so severe that pain reliever tablets, could not stop the pain anymore. Soon she arrived at the Dentist's office, and was seated in the waiting area. Through a small window on the wall, Lila soon noticed various teeth drilling tools hanging on the inside wall of the office. Lila panicked, but eventually calmed down.

She picked up some brochures and started reading as a way to calm down. She asked for the key to the ladies room. On her return from the ladies room she noticed some information on the wall behind her, which she missed the first time she walked in. She decided to read it this time. Here are the exact words she read. "Tooth may be extracted through the use of various instruments and methodists". Wait a minute Lila said in her mind. "If this Dentist does not even know the spelling of "methods", he is not going to treat me". Lila said her toothache soon vanished, and she walked out of the Dentist's Office and went home. I am certain Lila's pain would sooner or later return, but fear of Dentists is real as shown from this story. Thanks to passenger Lila.

Humor Story from Senegal

Adam is a friend of mine from Senegal, a Francophone country in West Africa. He currently lives in the United States. Occasionally he visits Senegal to see his parents and other relatives. Adam loves African cultural clothes, and on each trip he would add some more to his collection.

On one of his recent trips, he decided to have a local tailor make a few clothes for him. On this day, Adam went to the local market to buy the fabric for the tailor. African materials are usually very colorful so Adam had a wide variety of fabrics to choose from. Eventually he made his choices, and headed to the tailor's shop.

The time was near Christmas, and there are always a lot of people who go to the tailor's shop around that time of the year. When Adam got to his usual tailor, he already had a pile of work, and was not accepting any new work orders at that time. These are usually one-man tailor shops, so they can only produce a limited amount of work in time for the holiday festivities, when everybody needs their new clothes.

The tailor then suggested to Adam that he would send him over to his other tailor friend. Adam was directed to another tailor and he took his materials over to him.

This tailor warmly greeted him. He was a fairly older tailor, Adam thought, but he was quite experienced as a tailor. He had been sewing clothes for almost 50 years.

He showed Adam the various designs to chose from. Adam was browsing through the designs, to choose the particular style he wanted. You know Senegal is a French-speaking nation along with other native Senegalese dialects. Some people speak English language as well but most people are not very fluent with English. This poor older tailor was among the non-English speaking Senegalese, but as a tailor he often receive customers who only spoke English. In other to keep up with those English-speaking customers, he had many instructions hanging on the wall of his shop, in English.

Adam spoke both English and French very fluently, so he had no trouble with oral conversations with the tailor in French. But Adam was fascinated at the instructions on the wall, so he began reading them. Here is the exact thing Adam read "Bring your holiday materials early, before you know it, Christmas day will be here, we will execute customers in the order they arrive"

Adam looked around for machete but non-was around. He had the longest laugh of his life. The old man inquired why he was laughing, and Adam told him it was his sign on the wall, explaining to him the translation in French. The old man was surprised to learn that. He quickly took the signs down for good. Thank you Adam for this great story, I am happy that tailor did not execute you.

Chapter 32
Humor From Down Under

This story came from Joshua, a passenger from Australia. Once this project took off, I began to collect stories from as many passengers as I could. Humor stories happen all the time. They take place at times without people recognizing them. Joshua visited Chicago from Sidney in the Kangaroo country. He was a very funny man indeed.

He was in Chicago for a trade show at the Chicago convention center. He hired my taxi one evening to give him a small-guided tour of the windy city. We began the tour from his hotel-Hyatt on Printers row, on Dearborn Street. Joshua is a pretty religious person as can be seen from his name. He wanted to see some of the great cathedrals in Chicago.

The closest starting point was the "Old Saint Patrick" cathedral on Adams and Des Plaines in the loop. The tour took us through the loop to the Gold Coast, and Lincoln Park. I showed him Saint Michael's cathedral on Sedgwick Avenue. I also took him to the Holy name cathedral on State Street, as well as to the bishop's mansion. I asked him along the way if he had any humor stories to share with me. He was very happy to tell me the story of his small daughter and what happened on their way to the Church one Sunday morning. Her name is May.

Joshua and his wife regularly take her to church every Sunday. They live on the outskirts of Sidney, a large Australian city. On Sundays, Joshua would give her daughter some coins on their way to the church. Two coins total were always given to her. She is instructed to put one coin into the church collection plate. The other coin she would use to buy candy on their way home.

On this particular Sunday the family reached the church building few minutes early. They usually walk a few blocks from the place they parked their car. May was walking a few steps ahead of her parents with her two coins. She tripped and fell to the ground. She was fine though, but one of her coins rolled away from her hand.

She gave chase to the coin as it rolled away. Unfortunately for her, this coin dropped into the sewer hole. She heard it striking the bottom of the sewer system. May was very upset. Her parents walked up to her and asked her what the problem was. May said nothing momentarily. Tears were dropping from her eyes.

Joshua pulls her to his shoulders and gave her a kiss. He asked her again why she was crying. May showed Joshua the only remaining coin, pointing at the opening where the other coin fell. “Its okay” Joshua tells her, but May answered “No its not” Telling Joshua that it was God’s coin that got away from her. The remaining coin was her candy money May told her parents. Both of her parents laughed and told May that she should thank God for saving her candy money. Who says small children are not smart, well this story proves that fact.

Confession Of Sins

This story is about a woman who went to the Roman Catholic Priest to confess her sins. Roman Catholics have this process through which individuals every once in a while would see the Priest to confess their sins, the Priest would pray for them so their sins may be forgiven. The problem is that this particular woman’s voice is usually so loud that when she is talking to the priest, the other people in the church would hear her as well.

Repeated attempts by the Priest to get her to lower her voice failed. So the Priest came up with a unique solution. He asked this woman to write down her sins on a piece of paper, and hand it over to him when she attends confessions. She would start that on her next confession date.

A few weeks passed by and it was time for her to go to her next confession. So she sat down and did what the Priest suggested. She listed all her sins on a white sheet of paper. She decided to leave early so as to do her grocery shopping before going to the confession. This will enable her to catch up with the local grocery shop, which would close before she gets back from confessions.

So she sat down, and prepared a second list, on an identical paper to the list of her sins. She now left for the grocery store. Everything worked out fine and soon she completed her shopping and checked out. She pushed the cart to her car outside and loaded her groceries into the car. She realized that she was running late to the confession, so she horridly left. She left one of her lists inside the cart, taking the second list with her. She made it to the Priest okay, and patiently waited for her turn. Her turn had arrived, and she went into the confession booth. As soon as she walked into the booth, she handed the confession list the Priest requested, and knelt down before him.

The Priest opened the list and it was fairly long. On closer examination, the Priest asked her if she just went into a grocery store. She said yes. "Well this is a grocery list you gave me", the woman was embarrassed, and she quickly rushed back to the grocery store when she realized that she left the second list on the shopping cart.

When she got to the parking lot of the grocery shop, two boys gathering carts were already reading the list of her sins. She asked them what they were reading. One of the boys said it was a list of sins, and whoever committed those sins belonged in prison. The boys asked her, "You did all that"? She quickly grabbed the list from them and went back to the priest. Story was from Lisa, one of my passengers. Thanks a lot Lisa that was a good one.

Chapter 33
Brazilian Connections

My next story has a Brazilian twist to it, compliments of passenger Cody. Brazil has some of the best beaches in South America. A particular nudist beach attracts a few American nudists, from California. On a certain day, three nudists from the California area were vacationing at the beach. It was a long holiday weekend in the Unites States. The three men were executives of an Internet company, in the Los Angeles area.

As the name of the beach suggests, it is simply a nudist beach meaning that people at that beach are all supposed to be nude. But what happens when the President of the company recognizes his newly hired secretary approaching from the other direction? Well that was exactly what happened in this story.

As the three California nudists walked down the beach, the president saw his newly hired secretary in the distance. The other two men have not met this particular secretary before, so they had nothing to worry about. But the President had some problem here to deal with.

As the girls approached them, the other two men were a little bit shy because this was their first of such experience. The two men used their beach towels to wrap around their waist area. The President wrapped his towel around his face instead. The three girls soon passed them; the two men asked the President why he covered his face with the towel instead of his waist.

Well here is the explanation the president gave them. He said, "Well in the part of the country where I live, men are recognized from their faces instead of their waist". He never explained to his colleagues his real reason. A few weeks after that, one of the two men was having lunch inside the company cafeteria when the newly hired secretary walked up to him and said, "Hi, my name is Cindy". "Hi I am Rob" he replied. "So you work here," Cindy asked. "Yes" Rob said.

"Do you remember my face"? Cindy asked. Rob said no.

"I remember yours," said Cindy. "No way because I have never seen you before," Rob said. "Do you want me to remind you where I saw you"? Cindy asked, "Please do"

Rob added. "I saw you at the nudist beach in Brazil with two other guys, one of the guys covered his face with a towel". "Who is that guy, he has a very sexy body," Cindy added.

"Oh we just had his funeral", Rob told Cindy. "Oh I am sorry to hear that," Cindy replied.

Soon lunch was over and Cindy and Rob parted ways. Story came from one of my passengers, thanks Cody.

He Wont Take No For An Answer

It was the late days of November, and winter had begun to rear its ugly head in Chicago. I just picked up a fare to the Buck town area. The time was 2.30 am on late Friday night, and the late night bars were just beginning to close down in the city. My fare took me to Damen and Armitage area.

I had just dropped off my fare and about to head to Milwaukee and Division when I noticed a young woman running towards my taxi. She was partially naked. She literally ran into the taxi and told me to drive off immediately.

“Where are you going to”? I asked. “Please take me to Diversey and Seminary she said”. I took off immediately when I saw a man running out of a close by building from where the woman came from. Who is this man chasing us I asked? “I just escaped from his house,” she said.

Who is he? I asked. “I just met him at a bar and he convinced me to come with him to his apartment, and I did”. She further said that when they got to his apartment, he wanted to have sex with her. She objected on the ground that she just met him. This guy does not take no for an answer however, and was pretty determined to have his way.

He forcibly removed her clothes. But as soon as he walked into the bathroom, the lady opened the door and ran away from the house, leaving her blouse behind. “That is an attempted rape,” I said. “He was very drunk,” my passenger added. She also said she does not want to press any charges.

“Do you have any extra T-Shirt?” she asked. I told her, I have one in my trunk. All the time she was covering her breasts with her two hands. I went to the trunk and pulled out an extra T-shirt and gave her. She quickly slipped it on. Why would you follow a stranger like that home by 2.30 am? I asked her "I was just plain silly" she said, telling me that her two friends warned her not to go home with him.

"Well I hope you have learnt your lesson tonight". "You may not be as lucky next time," I added. What if I was not there at that particular time? I asked. "I think it was just an act of God," she said. A few more blocks we pulled up to her friend's apartment, my passenger asked me to honk and I did. Her friends came out of the apartment and paid for the fare. They also gave me an extra twenty dollars for the T-shirt. Not bad for the T-shirt I paid ten dollars for. The windy city is simply a lovely town where anything goes.

Chapter 34

Marijuana For Medical Treatment

Navy Pier is a busy fun place. It attracts both local residents and out of state tourists. One Friday night, I went there to solicit for passengers. The time was about 11 pm on a typical summer night in Chicago. The complex closes down about 11 pm on Fridays.

One hippy kind of guy walked up to me and asked if I could take him to Buck town. “Please come in,” I said. He entered the taxi and we took off. “Can I smoke”? He asked. I told him that it bothers me. “I have been working all day, and have not been able to smoke for a long time”, he told me. “If you let me smoke, he further said, I would give you a hefty tip”. “Well I will make an exception tonight,” I told him he could smoke on condition that he rolled his windows down.

He lights up something I thought was a cigarette, and rolled down the back windows to let the smoke out. We were heading in the direction of the freeway I 90/94 at this time. But the smell coming from the back seat was an unusual smoke. It did not smell like cigarette smoke I thought. What the hell is this guy smoking behind me I wondered?

He took a few more puffs, and I was pretty convinced that the smoke was not that of a cigarette. “What kind of cigarette are you smoking, it smells unusual,” I asked. “Good old Cools Menthol” he added. “Well this does not smell like Cools to me” I said. By now I had entered the expressway heading towards North Avenue. I waited for him to take another puff, to see for myself what this guy was smoking. Mentally I had figured out what he was smoking, but I had to confirm that, one way or another.

I watched him from my rearview mirror. I looked back momentarily, and saw a small narrow wrapped object in his mouth. It was Marijuana. “Sir, it is against the law to smoke marijuana inside a taxi”. I told him. “Why did you lie to me?” I asked. “Well it is for medical use,” he said. “What kind of medical use, this is not Oregon nor California, I don’t even think you can do that in those states anymore”.” My doctor prescribed it for pain” he told me, he stretched his hands to take another smoke, but I told him I was not going to continue on this trip if he did not put off the joint.

He puts off the joint, but had already smoked more than half of it anyway. I exited on North Avenue at this time. Is he going to still give me the hefty tip he promised me? Well only time would tell, but at that time I was not concerned with his tip. I could loose my license if the police stopped us.

A few more blocks, we turned right on Damen Avenue, and he asked me to pull off on Wabansia Avenue. It was a four-way stop, I did. Soon a police car flashed its green lights behind me. I panicked. My passenger quickly threw a twenty-dollar bill to me. The total fare was about eleven dollars. He horridly said, "keep the change" and vanished. The marijuana smoke still smelled in the taxi, I was worried that the cop might smell it.

The cop walked up to me and asked for my license. My heart was pounding faster. I gave him my license. "Let me see you Chauffer license also" he said. I quickly gave him that as well. He walked back to the squad car. A good break for me as I reached for a handy can of air freshener. I sprayed the entire contents in the taxi, making sure nothing was left in the can.

The officer soon walked back to me. He told me he was going to give me a warning this time." Next time, do not block an intersection to drop a passenger, always pull to the curbside," the officer told me. "Thanks officer", I said, and my pounding heart started to ease off at that moment. The officer bends over to give me back my licenses.

"Nice smelling taxi" he said. Thanks officer, "I did it all for you" I told him. Thank goodness the ordeal was finally over.

Chapter 35
What A Chicago Cabbie Can Do For You

You will be amazed at the level of service that some Chicago cabbies would provide to their passengers. A satisfied Chicago cab patron gave this story to me. Denis said she was pleasantly satisfied with this cab driver. That incident changed her views for Chicago cabbies, she thinks the driver in question was a very good ambassador for the company he worked for. Well I asked Denis what cab company he worked for. She did not remember, but said it was one of those long Cab Company names very hard to remember.

Obviously the cab driver in question must be an independent operator I thought. Here is the story that Denis told me. This driver picked her up from the Dominick's food store on Roosevelt Avenue. She had just finished shopping for groceries, and had over eight bags of grocery to carry. This nice cabbie took control of the situation, helping Denis to push her cart full of groceries to the point where the taxi was parked.

He carried the groceries one bag at a time. When Denis tried to help him, he asked her not to worry. The day in question was cold and breezy, if you have been to Chicago in mid January, you would better understand how nasty the winter blizzard conditions could be. So this cabbie told Denis, that she should let him do all the work. He walks her to the warm taxi, opened the door for her, and Denis was seated inside.

Eventually he finished loading the taxi with her groceries, and entered the taxi. Denis told him she was going to an address on South Dearborn Avenue. They drove off. It was a fairly short distance, and five minutes later, they arrived at her condo. The cabbie walked around to Denis' door, and opened the taxi door for her.

Denis walked out, while this guy unloaded her groceries into her building. He carried each bag to the entrance of the elevator. It was a high-rise building. Once he finished with that, Denis asked him how much the fare was. He told her it was about six dollars. Denis paid him ten dollars, a hefty tip. Denis expected him to leave then after he was paid, but he was not done yet.

The cabbie signaled the elevator, and carried all the groceries inside the elevator as well. He stepped out of the elevator, and waited for the door to close while smiling and waving good-bye to her. Well when Denis finished her story, I asked her, what did this nice cabbie do after the elevator left? "Did he leave the building or not"? Denis smiled and said she hope he left the building. Well you have seen for your self, a true story from a satisfied Chicago cab patron. When next you see a cab driver, treat him as a compassionate human being, which he is. Chicago cabbies are the best. Special thanks go to Denis for this testimonial.

Chapter 36
Strange Cargo

Ed was born in Adelaide Australia. He grew up there, and completed high school and college education, before he moved to the United States. He now lives in Chicago and he is a practicing attorney. He hired me to take him to the Comisky Park one evening to see the Chicago White Socks baseball game. Along the way, we exchanged humor stories.

Ed told me a taxi story from Australia. He drove taxi part-time while he lived in Sidney, and attended college. He told me a classic story about what happened to a fellow cab driver in a company where he worked. The company was fairly small; as such they handled funerals on a part-time basis to augment their taxi income.

This driver was newly hired, and usually new taxi drivers are tested when they join the company. The task for this poor guy was quite unusual. He was assigned to go to the morgue to pick up a body for a funeral. The instructions were simple and direct. "Enter the funeral through the back door, go straight to the second door to your right". He was further told that the body would be found on a table straight ahead, under white sheets.

His task was to transfer the body into a coffin under the table. A Porter is available on the second floor and he may signal him for assistance by pushing the button near the door. So this new driver set out for the assignment. He was neatly dressed in dark tuxedo, with bow ties. He had no trouble locating the funeral home. He parked the van next to the back door of the building and boldly walked towards the door. He sang along as he walked, obviously a sign of confidence and fearlessness. He opened the back door, automatically triggering the lights. The hall way was illuminated. A few quick steps he reached the second door on the right. As his hands approached the doorknob to open it, this door swung open, automatically.

The table stood in the center of the room. The opposite window was open, and light breeze was gently blowing across the room. As told, the body was lying on the table, covered in immaculate white sheets. There was calm and silence in the room you know the type of silence and tranquility found in burial grounds.

He momentarily stopped singing. He pulls up the white sheet covering the body, but the sheet fell out of his hands back to its former position. He took a few steps back. He summoned up some courage and moved back towards the body again. The cabbie tries a second time and this time the sheets stayed opened.

He looked at the body. It was a man, and his face muscle seemed to have contracted a little and he seemed to be smiling. He closed the sheets back, and chill began to run down his spine. The straw that broke the camel's back was when the white sheet began shaking as if the body underneath was attempting to sit up. This poor guy's hair grew a few inches taller.

His face turned pale, and his jaw dropped. He tried to control his aggravated fear but to no avail. Suddenly his lips unleashed an almighty scream as he ran faster than a speeding bullet, bumping his head on the door as he ran. He jumped into the mini van and took off. When he reached the office of the Taxi Company, he parked the taxi, and told the dispatcher that he is quitting. He drove home and this incident effectively ended his hopeful career as a taxi driver. The funeral was rescheduled for another day. Thanks to passenger Ed, for this great story.

Chapter 37
Inspiring The Young

The next story arouses compassion to its fullest, the young child's way. As part of her religious inspiration a certain Chicago parent decided to take their young daughter named Janet to a Christian art exhibition at a small art gallery in Chicago. When they reached the exhibition hall, they started at the beginning point of the display, as they walked down the hallway.

The parents explained along the way the exhibitions to their daughter. Janet liked that and was very inquisitive to learn the details of the art. Soon the parents reached an exhibition showing how Christians were persecuted for their Christian beliefs. The particular painting had images of Christians being thrown to the lion's den. It also showed how the lions were devouring the body of the Christians.

So Janet's parents explained those details to her as she intensely looked at those lions in the painting. But Janet's face was gradually changing. She looked a little sad. She still looked at those lions in the painting. "What's the matter"? Janet's mom asked her. Janet said nothing to her. "Hello Sweetie" her dad said to her, "what is wrong"?

By now tears started to drop from the young Janet's eyes. "It's those pictures," Janet pointed to the painting with the lions devouring Christians. Dad explains that those things happened years ago, and does not happen anymore. But it was not why young Janet was sad. "Well can you tell me why you are sad"? Her dad asked her. Something else had to be the problem he thought. Finally Janet told her parents that she was sad because the big lions in the painting were too busy eating all the Christians, and the baby lions had no Christians left to eat.

Her dad carried her in his arms, re-assuring her that the baby lions would be all right too. He calmed young Janet down as they continued with the exhibition. This goes to prove a point I have always known- Young children are very caring and compassionate.

Greatest Scare Of My taxi Career

This incident scared me like nothing else ever did. In fact I was dumbfounded by the incident for a few seconds. One winter evening, I answered a radio dispatcher announcement for a pick-up from an address on the Westside. I was just returning from a drop off in the area when the announcement was made. I generally don't hang around the Westside, but I often take fares to such destinations.

I went to check up the address. It was a small neighborhood bar. The name of the passenger to pick up was Mr. Johnson. He was standing at the door when I arrived. An elderly man, Mr. Johnson had been drinking for a while. "Are you Mr. Johnson"? I asked him "Yes" he said. He started walking towards the taxi. "Do you need some assistance?" I asked." "No I am fine," he told me. Well I cautioned him to be careful, reminding him that the ground was slippery. A few dusting of snow had fallen covering the snow already on the ground.

I barely finished saying that, when Johnson took a few wild steps, and landed on the pile of snow on the pavement. "Are you okay" I asked him, rushing towards him. "I am fine, it happens all the time", he said. By now I approached him and held him on his right arm as he stood up. "You drank a little too much," I said. His breath smelled with alcohol.

I managed to help him to the taxi. He sat down, and told me to take him to an address ten blocks away. Five minutes later we reached his destination. I was not going to allow a repeat of his previous fall, so I quickly stepped around the back door to assist him to the doorstep of his home.

He paid me about five dollars for the fare, and came out of the taxi. I grabbed his left arm as we walked to his doorstep. I noticed that his hand was stiff at that time, but I did not put too much thought into that. Mr. Johnson told me that he enters through the side door. That meant that we would walk through the grass to get there. "Whatever" I said.

So we walked across a pile of snow. This time I grabbed his stiff arm strong enough so as to avoid another fall. He was not walking straight, obviously the booze was impairing his ability to walk in a straight fashion. Suddenly, he slipped again and was falling down the second time. But I decided to stop him from hitting the ground, so I managed to hold his arm tight enough to prevent that.

What happened next scared me to death. Still grabbing his arm, Mr. Johnson's body separated from his hand, and he hit the ground. His arm popped out, and was still in my hands. I did not know what to do next, but there was no blood anywhere. He had lost one hand, and I was afraid to grab the other hand. His wife soon opened the door. She walked straight to me and said, "Don't worry young man". She took the artificial arm from me, and said, "This arm comes out often", and pretty soon he will loose it for good.

She handed it to someone in the house, and helped Mr. Johnson to the house. I breathed a sigh of relief and walked back to my taxi. What a day it was indeed.

Chapter 38
He Fooled Me

What do you do when a passenger pleads with you that he does not have enough money to pay for the fare, swearing that the last money with him was for the family dinner? Well this was my experience with this Passenger. I picked him up at the loop near Harrison and State streets. He pleaded with me that he was down to his last few dollars, and has run out of his unemployment compensation benefits. A big lie I thought he just made up.

We had already started the trip, and had gone about half the distance before he informed me that he doesn't have enough money to pay me. "Why did you take the taxi"? I asked him "I have an emergency at home" he claimed. It was a dilemma for me to resolve. "What emergency" I asked him "My wife is in an emergency" he said. "Well are you a doctor"? I asked him; if she is in an emergency, just call an ambulance. "They would get there before you." I reasoned.

He was going to 2400 block of west Jackson Avenue, near Western Avenue. He told me he had only five dollars to spend on the ride. The fare would have cost him about ten dollars. So I decided to give him a break, since he could pay half of the amount.

About ten minutes later, we arrived at his destination. He directed me to stop him on the corner near a liquor store. I pulled up and parked. The fare was about ten dollars and fifty cents. Johnson gave me five dollars, thanking me for my help. He told me the rest of his money would be used to buy his family dinner. I wished him well and left.

I drove away into a one-way street to turn around. I did not realize the street was a dead end. So I turned into another street, which was a dead end as well. I managed to find my way back to the liquor store where I dropped my passenger. As I pulled out in front of the liquor store, I saw Mr. Johnson, grabbing a case of Budweiser. I honked at him to make sure he saw me. We made eye contact and I pulled up to him.

"I thought you said you were broke Mr. Johnson" I asked him. He smiled. "Obviously your wife and young children would feed on Budweiser tonight," I inquired from him "You did not fool me Mr. Johnson, I never believed you in the first place" I told him. He was still smiling. "What about your wife's emergency, oh Bud would cure her" I am always pissed when people play on my intelligence, but what can I do this is city life, I reasoned.

Chapter 39

Inside Taxi Conversations

During the course of collecting stories to be included in this book, I uncovered some plot by a convention attendee. The extent this lady was willing to go, in other to avoid sex with her husband would surprise you. The following story was in- taxi conversation between three convention passengers I picked up from the McCormick convention center in Chicago. Cab drivers love interesting in- taxi conversations. All taxi passengers are hereby warned that even if your cab driver appears un-interested in your conversations, he is listening to them, particularly if the story has anything to do with sex.

Taxis line up at the McCormick Convention Center where my passengers for this story were picked up

She flew in from Philadelphia for the Hardware Convention in Chicago. The conversations the women had that day, was about sexual satisfaction a somewhat odd conversation for out of town convention attendees. It appeared that all three women were not happy with their sexual partners, who ever they may be. As the women exchanged their experiences, it was apparent to me that my three passengers simply don't get satisfaction from their partners. It was an interesting conversation, so I listened to the particular story from the lady from Philadelphia.

Here is the story she told her colleagues. She claimed that a typical sex encounter with her partner lasts for a maximum of two minutes. There was a long laugh from the other two ladies. One of the ladies assures the narrator that she is not alone. Her frustrations she claimed eventually led her to develop strategies to deal with the situation temporarily. I was not sure from her story if her partner was her husband or not. He may very well be her husband I concluded, because if he was just a boyfriend, one may ask why she couldn't just walk away. You may reach a different conclusion than I did however.

This passenger told her friends that her strategy worked well because her partner drinks. She made it clear that he was not an alcoholic. He would ordinarily have a maximum of three or four beers but could not handle much more than that. If he drank more than four, she said it makes him sleepy and drowsy. Her strategy was to get him sleeping before her so as to avoid sex with him. She accomplishes this goal by offering him a few more bottles, which according to her, does the trick.

She then starts to implement her delay tactics. She would ask him to wait for her, to take shower. He would lie down on the bed waiting for her unending shower. She cracks the bathroom door waiting for sleeping signals from him; and she stays in the shower until she hears him snoring. As soon as that happens, she would get out from the shower and gently lay down on the other side of the bed for a peaceful night sleep.

Her friends laughed, and promised her, they would try her tricks with their partners. Wait a minute, I said to her. Please pardon me for interfering in your conversation, you mean you would drug your husband to avoid sex with him? "No" she said, explaining further that he promised to see a sex councilor, until that happens, she would avoid having sex with him. The other women concurred with that, and I could not win the argument anyway, so I decided to shut-up, after all I was not part of the conversation anyway. I thought it was a silly strategy however.

Chapter 40
Supporting The Homeless

Chicago has its share of the homeless. Often you can see them on street corners. Many of them are struggling to make their lives better. Some sell "Streetwise Newspapers" to survive. Others would simply beg on the streets. Some of the homeless love cab drivers. I guess cab drivers are little more generous than the average citizen, I imagined. Many of the homeless would stand on cab lines waiting for cabbies. There is an explanation for that. Many of the Chicago cabbies are Muslims. Muslims are required to give assistance to the poor, a Muslim friend told me. So beggars know that, and would flock around cab stands to beg.

I very often give money to the homeless. But there is so much one can do. There are hundreds of the homeless in the loop. Many would beg you two or three times a day. They also don't understand that there are hundreds of other beggars like them. As such it is impossible to give each and everyone of them money all the time.

There is a particular homeless beggar at the sears tower cabstand. He has walking disabilities. Every time a taxi pulls up, he walks to the driver to ask for money. If the driver comes back to the same line for another fare, he would beg him again. When he is approaching the driver he often puts a performance for the driver, thereby highlighting his walking disabilities.

When he finally gets to the driver, he would ask, "You got a quarter maybe" Many times I do give him money. Usually fifty cents, because by the time I do that a few times it adds up. Many other drivers do give him money as well. Sometimes when he approaches me for the second or third time, I do remind him that I just gave him money a few minutes ago. But that does not matter because his strategy is to beg each taxi on the line.

One day I asked him what he does with all the money he collects every day. He told me that all his money is for food. We were just exchanging some words because it was slow that day. "About how much money do you collect per day "? I inquired. "About Sixty dollars" he told me. Not bad for a daily income I said, and all this income is tax-free too, he laughs. "And you said all your money is spent on food"? I inquired, "Yes" he said. "You must be feeding on caviars", I asked him. I gave him fifty cents and left to pick up my fare.

Later that same day, I had a fare with a passenger who was running late. Everybody in Chicago is always in a hurry any way, so I don't pay much attention when passengers say that. But traffic was pretty bad that day so I decided to cut through an alley. I turned into this alley connecting Jackson and Van Buren streets.

As soon as I made that turn, I saw this homeless beggar sitting on the corner. His girlfriend, I assumed homeless as well, was also seated next to him. In between them were a pack of cigarette and a fairly large bottle of Vodka. As I drove by, I slowed down and said hi to him, making sure that he noticed me. He smiled as I drove by him.

The purpose of the story is not to undermine the problems of the homeless. They do need help of course but this story shows how human they are as well. The next time I saw this beggar; I still gave him my little token of support, but I also told him that I saw him with his girlfriend, a pack of cigarette and a large bottle of Vodka in the alley the other day. He came up with a wild explanation, saying his girl friend made him buy all that. I told him that I did not buy that, but I was not going to tell anyone about that. He smiled.

Chapter 41

Lead, Follow, Or Get Out Of My Way

This story is on a subject that you are quite familiar with-Sports Utility Vehicles.

SUV mania seems to be in the air. Just about everyone I know want to own them. They are quite comfortable and roomy as well. Don't get me wrong I like them as well, but some of the narrower ones are dangerous. The problem is that their "center of gravity" makes them susceptible to "rollovers"

Part of this problem also is the "road warrior mentality" of their owners. Many of them often hide behind a false sense of security. Chicago winters could be brutal at times. Hazardous driving conditions may develop in minutes. This day was no different. Chicago had just received about five inches of snow. Driving conditions were deteriorating. Salt trucks have all been deployed along the high ways and major streets.

Temperature was about two degrees. I had just picked up a passenger going to the Southside. On the Dan Ryan expressway traffic was slow because of the hazardous road conditions. Many veteran drivers know that such slippery road conditions require caution. Many of the vehicles on the road were driving slow, about ten to fifteen miles per hour.

I was doing about twenty miles per hour, which I considered the maximum safe speed one can do under the developing inclement whether conditions. But the traffic rolled along smoothly.

Out of nowhere came this SUV driver. It was a Chevy Blazer, one of those narrower SUVs. This guy was doing about forty to forty-five miles an hour. This is a clear case of "road warrior mentality" I talked about earlier. At that point we were approaching a curve where the local lanes are separated from the express lanes.

I knew immediately that this guy couldn't negotiate this curve with such speed under the prevailing road conditions. But his 4x4 mentality was pushing him along. He honked his horn and I simply cleared out of his way. As he attempted to negotiate the curve, his Blazer skidded, as he hit his brakes. His vehicle brushed on the side of an embankment and rolled over, with its four tires facing the sky.

Every body stopped. We rushed to help him. Miraculously he crawled out of the vehicle unhurt. "Are you okay" I asked him. He replied, "I am fine". The problem now was that his Blazer was blocking all the lanes, causing a massive traffic jam on Dan Ryan. I was caught in the middle of it all.

Well, it was his turn to get out of my way now I reasoned. The tow truck soon arrived to remove the Blazer. Traffic began to flow again. Lesson for all you SUV owners, Chicago's winter conditions require reason and commonsense.

Chapter 42
Is It Something You Ate

This story is about dating. It involves two lovers who went to an expensive restaurant. My anonymous passenger from Tampa shared the story with me. Two lovers went out for a date. His name is Rob and she is Tina. Tina has a very sophisticated taste. She suggested a particular upscale restaurant. Rob grudgingly agreed.

They got to the restaurant and were seated. Soon a waitress passed on the menu. Tina made her selection from the list. She passed the menu to Rob, he asked her to order for him as well. So Tina ordered the same dish again. Appetizers were soon served. “What type of wine do you all like Italian or French”? The waitress asked. “Whatever my sweetie wants,” Rob said. Don Per yon Tina requested.

Their dishes were soon brought. The food was delicious as Tina and Rob enjoyed the meal very much. They washed it down with a bottle of Don Per Yon. They were very satisfied and pleased with the quality of the meal. The waitress brought the bill and Tina passed it on to Rob.

Rob turned the bill over. The total bill was a hundred and ninety dollars excluding tips. Rob's eyes bulged out. He reached for his eyeglasses, thinking his sight was failing him. He read the same amount again. He had just enough to pay the bill. Tina came up with a fifteen-dollar tip.

Few minutes after Rob paid the bill, he complained of stomach upset. Tina asked, "Rob dear, what's the matter"? Rob said nothing, but was still grabbing his stomach. "Should I call the ambulance"? Tina asked. Rob said "No". "Is it something you ate or something I ate"? Tina asked. Rob assured Tina it was something she ate which caused his upset stomach.

Breast Implant Story

John was always teasing his wife about her small breasts. At first Emily did not take him serious, but when she realized that John had a preference for larger breasts, she wanted to do something about that. She consulted with a Plastic Surgeon, who suggested a breast implant.

Emily however wanted to surprise John, by not telling him about the operation. She came up with a plan. John occasionally goes out of town for business. So Emily planned to do the surgery on John's next business trip. She informed the Surgeon about the date she would like to have the operation. Every thing was set for that day.

Two weeks later John left town for his business trip. Emily went in for the operation. It was pretty smooth and in a few days she returned home. Emily was quite pleased with the operation, although she felt her breasts were slightly larger than the size she actually wanted. But anyway it's over now she thought.

Meanwhile Emily's friends complimented her on the operation assuring her that she looked good in her upper chest area. John called Emily to tell her, he is on his way back. Emily was excited and looked forward to that. John finally returned. He returned at night, and Emily was already on the bed.

John unlocks the door and walked into the house. He walked into the bed room, and said "Hi Honey" "Hi " Emily replied. "I have a surprise for you" Emily said. "What surprise" John asked. Emily was still under the blanket and John had not seen her new breasts yet. "Turn out the lights" Emily said.

John flips the light off. Emily moves the blanket over. She now said to John, "Turn the light on and look at my breast" John turns the light on, and shouted, “Oh my goodness, do you have anything smaller”? They laughed for quite sometime. Story came from one of my lady passengers from New York. I love New York.

Chapter 43
Ride Of Her Life

Kathy was picked up at Montrose and Ashland heading to the loop. She told me that she had an experience of her life recently. “What was it”? I asked her. Here is the story she told me. One day she was running late to work. It was a day that she could not afford to get to work late. On that day, she had to be present at a business meeting. Her boss warned her the previous week, to be on time for that meeting.

Unfortunately for her, she forgot to set her alarm before she went to sleep. She woke up fifteen minutes late and had to rush things that morning. She waited for taxi on the corner of Montrose and Ashland, and hoped to catch a cab soon. That day there were few cabs around. There was a big convention at the loop and most cabs were tied up there she found out later.

When she finally caught a cab, she had only fifteen minutes to be at the office. So this Checker guy pulls up. She quickly jumped in, and told the driver her problem. The driver was promised an extra ten-dollar tip, if he could make it to the loop in fifteen minutes. The driver told her “No problem” He asked Kathy to put on her seat belt. Kathy thought that was unusual for a cab driver to ask their passenger to belt up. She snatched up her seat belt and the flight to the loop was on.

This trip generally takes about twenty-five minutes because of the morning rush hour. Kathy did not realize what she just signed onto; when she offered this guy a ten-dollar tip. Some other drivers, may tell you that they would try, if you offered them a decent tip, but this guy simply gave her a guarantee that she would be in her office in fifteen minutes or less. He took off in a cloud of smoke, as his tires robbed off the pavement. Kathy said she smelt a burning tire when this driver took off.

He accelerated to speeds of up to sixty miles an hour on Ashland Avenue. Normal speed limit on Ashland is about thirty to thirty-five miles an hour. He slows down on red lights, and would look to the right and left basically watching for police cars. If he did not spot any, he drives through the red light. He did that for the next five lights. Kathy was thrown from one side of the taxi to the other. She held on to the bullet proof partition after the driver flew over a bump and Kathy’s head hit the roof of the taxi.

Kathy panicked so much that she started begging him to slow down, re-assuring him that she would still give him the ten dollar tip regardless of what time they made it to the loop. But this driver would not take any chances He flew over another pothole. The pothole had some water in it because it just rained. Water was flushed out, as it splashed on the window of another car on the adjacent lane, barely missing the driver.

Meanwhile Kathy said she prayed for a few seconds. This driver cruised down Ashland to Clyburn Avenue, cutting through a few alleys. He busted out onto Chicago Avenue, down to Kingsbury Avenue into the loop. Kathy had survived. She quickly got out of the taxi and paid him, including the ten-dollar tip she promised him.

The entire trip took less than fifteen minutes. Kathy made it into the office three minutes before nine o'clock; the meeting was the farthest thing on her mind at that point. She only was concerned with surviving the ride. Well when she finished the story, I told her that she got what she asked for. You've got to love Chicago cabbies.

Chapter 44
Short Mini Skirt Story

One summer afternoon, I picked up a passenger on the corner of Randolph and State Street. She was shopping, and just came out of the Marshal Field's Department Store. She had a few shopping bags, along with her handbag, and a cell phone. She wore an unusually short mini red skirt, barely longer than her butts. But two guys standing on the corner seem to like what they saw, as they admired her.

She got into the Taxi and asked me to take her to the Saks Fifth Avenue store on Michigan Avenue. She told me that she just moved to Chicago from Milwaukee. Along the way we had some brief conversation. She asked me what I thought about her dress because it seemed like men were taking an extended look at her. I was caught unawares by that one; I had to quickly come up with an answer.

Chicago's magnificent mile near Water Tower Mall and Saks Fifth Avenue where the lady was dropped off

"Chicago men love short women," I told her. "Wait a minute, do you mean I am short"? She asked. "No I meant to say that Chicago men love short outfits", I told her. The fact remains that she is short as well.

"Why do Chicago men love short dresses?" she further asked me.

"I am not exactly sure, it could be the nice legs, or lack of it" that gets people's attention

"Are you saying my legs are nice or not" she asked me "Oh I did not look at your legs. I will look at them on your way out. I promised to give her thumbs up or down depending on what I thought.

Soon we got to Saks Fifth avenue store. Her cell phone rang. She answered her phone briefly promising the caller to call back in a few minutes. She paid me for the fare. I had already promised myself, that the answer I would give her about what I thought of her legs would only depend on one thing -how much tip she gave me. She was quite generous with her tip however. Yes you are right if you think that cab drivers are obsessed with tips.

She stepped out of the taxi, and posed for me. I gave her thumbs up. But she does have a nice set of legs though. As she turned back, still grabbing her shopping bags, handbag and cell phone, her cell phone fell to the ground. She attempted to reach for it but realized that her dress was way too short. When she tried to pick up the phone the first time, her underwear was exposed, so she quickly stood back up without picking up her phone.

One male pedestrian noticed the unfolding mini-drama, and decided to get a little entertainment out of the scene. I attempted to come out of the taxi to help her, but traffic was too heavy for me to open the driver door, without another car ripping it off. She was determined not to entertain this on looking guy however.

Obviously she may have practiced the acrobatic show she was about to put up. She slipped off her right shoe, and grabbed the antenna section of her cell phone with her toes, flipping it up in the air, and finally caught it with her right hand. She then slipped her foot back into her shoe. She looked at me one more time; I gave her a second thumbs up. She smiled and dashed into the Saks Fifth Avenue store. I finally moved on.

Chapter 45
English Humor Story

For some reason cab drivers usually know many humor stories. Part of the reason is the nature of taxi work. Tap on any former taxi driver and ask for taxi stories, and you will hear some good ones. Tim drove taxi as well in London while he sought his accounting certification. Taxi occupation as difficult and dangerous as it may be, is a good job for students. It offers a very flexible schedule, and a fairly decent income.

My passenger lives in Rolling Meadows now, and works for a prestigious Chicago accounting firm. One evening, Tim got out of work late, and he decided to take a taxi home to his suburban Chicago residence. Normally, he takes the suburban Metra train.

Along the way we exchanged stories. He told me about his cab stories from London.

He was once dispatched to pick up an older man from the Pub. His passenger had been drinking for some time. He requested Tim to take him to a Fishing Quay to pick up his fishing boat. It was not a long trip, and Tim was not particularly pleased with that. But any way he set out with his passenger.

The Quay was soon sighted. His passenger asked him to pull up as close as he could to the curb. Tim pulled within a few inches to the edge of the Quay. The fare was about three English pounds, less than five dollars. His passenger exited the taxi, and Tim thought he wanted to get out, so as to reach in his pocket to pay the fare.

This passenger simply vanished. Tim looked around and he was simply nowhere to be found. Tim was very upset. His passenger filled his taxi with alcohol breath. The trip was very short, and now he was not going to be paid, because the passenger had run away. Tim called his dispatcher and made a report of the incident.

He walked out of the taxi and, noticed two people standing on the far corner of the Quay. One of them was pointing to the water and he walked close to them to find out what they were looking at. He looked down also and saw his drunken passenger in the water holding on to the edge of the platform. Tim then realized what happened. This passenger on stepping out of the taxi, not knowing that Tim pulled up so close to the edge of the Quay in addition to him being drunk, fell into the water.

By now the police had arrived as well. Tim explained to the police what happened. His passenger was dragged out of the water. He took in some water when he fell in but he was okay. He paid the fare with a wet currency and Tim finally left.

Chapter 46
Dispatcher Humor Story

One of the small cab companies in Chicago was having a little theft problem. An assistant to the dispatcher usually order one dozen fresh doughnuts in the morning. He eats two pieces with his morning coffee, and passes out half a dozen to the mechanics in the garage shop, and saves the remaining four doughnuts for late afternoon snack.

For about five days in a roll, one of the mechanics from the workshop steals the remaining doughnuts. When the assistant dispatcher confronted the mechanics, all of them denied stealing the leftover doughnuts. Repeated attempts failed to stop the donought theft. Well the dispatcher concluded that they had a rodent problem in the building.

He came up with a unique solution to deal with the problem. He bought another dozen doughnuts the following day and saved his extra four doughnuts, but this thief or rodent ate the left over doughnuts again. So this dispatcher got on the intercom and made the following announcement. "Today's doughnuts were laced with rat poison, it would cure the rodent problem in the building; hopefully the missing doughnuts were not eaten by humans, in case it was, whoever ate them, would need to go to the hospital immediately"

There was hysteria in the garage. Every mechanic looked at each other to see if anyone would come forward, but nobody did. A few minutes later, a certain mechanic walked into the men's room. He was heard attempting to vomit something, but he was unsuccessful.

He soon came out of the rest room, and walked out of the building, and was heard screaming as he ran on the street, "I have been poisoned, somebody get me an ambulance". When the dispatcher heard that, he got on the intercom again and said that the earlier announcement he made was just a joke.

Other employees ran outside to fetch the mechanic who ate the doughnuts. He was informed that the announcement was not true, and the doughnuts were not poisoned. From that day, his doughnuts were left alone.

Anthrax Story

During the anthrax scare in the United States, following September eleven tragedy, many people were worried about the possibility of anthrax infection. People were worried enough that some people got prescriptions of the anti biotic called Cipro, which was promoted as the most effective antibiotics for anthrax.

One of my passengers hired me to take him to get a prescription of Cipro.This passenger was in his late sixties I thought. He wanted me to wait and take him back home. There were a few other individuals waiting for the same purpose. The doctor's assistant passed out some warning memo of the possible side effects of Cipro.I was waiting for my passenger inside the doctor's office as well.

The warnings stated, "Do not take Cipro if you are, or suspect to be pregnant, no alcoholic beverages; limit coffee consumption to a maximum of two cups a day; Cipro may cause headaches, nausea, fever, swelling on the face, kidney damage and liver damage, epilepsy and on and on.

When my passenger finished reading the list of possible side effects of Cipro, he walked to the doctor and asked him if it was true that Cipro could cause all the listed side effects, the doctor said yes. He told the doctor, "Well I would rather have anthrax than these side effects, at least anthrax is curable, but some of the side effects are not" He asked me to take him home, and left the doctor's office.

Chapter 47

Perspectives on African Funerals

One morning I picked up a passenger from the Midway airport who was heading to Rogers Park. The look on her face was a testament that something was wrong. She looked very sad, and I wondered if I should ask her, what the problem was.

I thought for a few moments about that, because I did not want to aggravate her condition any further.

After I drove a few blocks, I noticed that she was crying.

At that point I asked her what the problem was. My question actually made her cry louder than before. My goodness, I thought that I just made matters worse for her. What can I do to comfort this passenger, who was also a total stranger to me? Soon after this thought flashed through my mind, my passenger told me she was sorry to disturb me. She introduced herself as Jane, telling me further that she came to Chicago for her brother's funeral. I was sorry to hear that I told her. At the time, I just returned from my brother's funeral in Africa, as a matter of fact I was still going through the grief and pain of his untimely death. I told Jane that I truly understand what she was going through, assuring her that as painful as death is, she would overcome the grief in the near future.

She further told me that her brother that died was her only brother, and his death was so untimely that she did not have a chance to say good-bye to him. He was involved in a motorcycle accident, stressing further that she was against him buying a motorcycle.

He died on the way to the hospital. At this point she began to cry again and I decided to comfort her, by telling her of a similar experience I had when my brother passed away suddenly. My passenger momentarily stopped crying and asked me to please share the story with her.

Here is the detailed story of my brother's funeral as I told Jane.

One may ask why do I want to relive the pain of talking about my brothers' death?

My answer to this is quite simple, by writing about it; I am dealing with the pain at the same time. Death is an inevitable end and should be dealt with, as one of the processes of life. Nobody has ultimate control over this process and the best that modern medical technology could do is to prolong the process of life.

This is a story about the day my brother passed away. Even as I tell this story, I am fighting to hold down tears despite the fact that it has been a few years since his untimely death, but he was a good man and in the Ibo culture, death as painful as it is, should be celebrated.

I saw him last, about three years before his death, but I spoke with him regularly, in fact I remember very vividly that he requested that I buy him a cell phone on my next trip to Africa. He had just bought a Mercedes car and wanted to equip it with a cell phone to facilitate his busy business schedule.

I lived in Chicago Illinois at the time. I had just finished the days' work, and arrived home at about three am in the morning. I opened the door of my apartment and there were some friends and relatives sitting alongside my roommate.

I wondered why they had gathered in my apartment at this time of the morning.

So I inquired what was wrong? There was silence in the room. I asked again, can someone tell me what happened as I started to imagine what the problem could have been. I walked to the window and drew open the window blind and started looking at a wonderful and peaceful blue skies full of shining stars.

Within a split second, I saw the brightest star in the sky fall out of its orbit, and soon disappeared in the horizon. I asked myself what was the significance of that, but the answer was becoming obvious. My interpretation of what I just saw was that, the brightest star represented a member of my family, and the analogy was that when the star fell out of the skies, it signified some kind of bad news in my family, involving a senior family member.

As I turned around from the window a friend walked to me, and held my hands, he told me, "your brother has just passed away".

It is hard to describe the first feelings, but I remember being in total darkness momentarily. I asked how could this be? Uche said," we received a message from Africa confirming the story".

I was very confused and did not know what to do next, but I soon realized that this is the time to show some strength. It is now my turn to assume the leadership role in the family, reassuring the entire family that things will be alright.

African funerals are not just death; it is also a celebration of the life the individuals lived. As Stephen Buckley of the Washington Post said," Funerals are not just ordinary on the African continent, far from being morbid, funerals are seen as a celebration of the dead."

I regained my composure from the initial shock, which I received over his death, and soon my attention was drawn to the daunting job of organizing the traditional burial rights. African funerals are very comprehensive and detailed compared to funerals in the U.S

But how can I effectively organize this burial from Chicago, there was also the consideration that as an elder with social standing, his funeral would require more planning.As a member of the Ibo tribe, there are many details that needed to be ironed out, so I began planning a trip back to Africa. I kept in touch with the rest of the family, and informed them that I, would soon be on the way.

Meanwhile the Ibo Community in Chicago was very helpful in pitching in with some generous donations towards the funeral arrangements. The one pattern that will continue to manifest in African life and culture is the way communities rely on each other to solve all of its problems. That culture still survive among the African community here in the United States.

Like Hilary Clinton's " It takes a village" theme in discussing African communal life, well this funeral would actually take more than a village.

Soon the financing was put together and I was on the way back to Nigeria. I soon arrived at my hometown, Abatete, a town on the outskirts of Onitsha, a commercial center in Anambra State of Nigeria.

A plan was put in place to keep the news away from my aged mother, until I got back because nobody knew how she would react. I arrived at the village at about 7 pm in the evening, As soon as I entered the house, I walked to my mothers' room to greet her. We talked for a few minutes as the crowd began to swell on the news that I had returned.

The village Chiefs and elders were also gathering on the news of my arrival. We had to tell mom the dreaded news because the numbers of people streaming into the compound continued to increase. And I was anxious to get this information out to her so we may proceed with the planning of the funeral.

In the company of my three sisters, we took mom to the inner room and broke the news to her while assuring her that, things would work out fine.

The news hit her hard, but the plan worked because in the company of her children she was able to absorb the shock fairly quickly meanwhile, the actual funeral planning had begun.

I had a quick meeting with the elders about the strategies and details of the burial. About 50 people would spend the night inside the compound and they would all be fed for that night, but I was prepared. Soon the gospel singers arrived, followed by the youth choir and the celebration had begun.

It was a continuous singing and dancing all night long,

At cockcrow in the morning, we started to implement our strategies for the funeral.

A lot of the people in the village generally rely on cockcrow as an early morning wake-up call. Don't get me wrong, African towns do have watches, and clocks and satellite dishes as well, but some culture still survive the global cultural imperialism.

This is part of the life in the village, to wake up at cockcrow, if one has an early duty to perform.

So the day's activities had started, for that day, a group of about fifteen women were assigned to go to the market to buy food for the day, estimate was for about 1000 people.

A group of young men about ten in number were also asked to go and buy a cow, to be slaughtered, on their return. Another group of five men were in charge of the Palm wine {local wine tapped from palm tree, high in alcohol}

The day began in earnest and there were many bands ranging from choir, to traditional dance groups. It was a big day, the day that my brother's body would be brought home from the Morgue.

The highlight of the day was when the funeral procession arrived at the compound. There was a ceremonial 24-gun salute as people came in to pay their last tributes. This was the first opportunity for me to catch a glimpse of my brother's remains, as his casket was opened. He was very peaceful indeed.

There was an open air mass attended by a Roman Catholic Priest. My brother was laid to rest on the South-east corner of our compound next to our fathers grave, as masquerade dancers performed.

The celebration continued into the night, but the burial marked the the beginning point for the traditional dances, many groups would participate in this stage of the festivities.

The first group of dancers to take the stage was the members of my brother's age grade. They were about 40 in number. Age grades are common among the Ibo tribesmen, it is an all men club, and the members of the club have one thing in common; they were born on or about the same year.

Their dance was very good; they had two masquerades and several drummers. Tradition has it that the first son of my late brother, would be bestowed with the title recognizing him as the inheritor of their father's crown, a type of " rites of passage ceremony" So we called on his first son to join in the dance. A shy young man in his late tens, he put up a not so shy performance , to the cheers of the crowd.

Soon it was my turn to do the traditional dance as the new head of the extended family.

Members of my brother's age grade doing their traditional burial dance at the funeral

There was an expectation that I may not do the traditional dance, because I have been living in the United States for too long, but I proved them all wrong as I took control of the floor amid cheers of

"Son of the soil" For me it was an experience I would cherish for a long time to come.

Traditional chiefs in their traditional regalia take turns as they pay their tribute to my brother

The traditional dance continued as my late brothers' kids, took their turn.

The performance of a two-year-old child who came out of the crowd and joined in the dance, was a great tribute to my brother indeed.

Everybody that came to the funeral was served food and drinks. Alcohol was served to mostly men and adults. Some women were served with alcohol as well. An estimate of about three thousand people came to our compound during the three-day ceremony, to pay their last tribute to my brother.

The ceremony was marked with pomp and pageantry as women groups perform at the funeral

It was now time for me to thank the attendees in appreciation of their efforts. I would add that many African funerals offer individuals the opportunity to contribute towards the cost of the burial, in some cases, it may be possible to raise a small portion of the total cost of the funeral.

At last it was time for me to take a night rest having been awake for more than forty-eight hours, but I had one more encounter with my brother in a dream, he showed up by the window of my room, he was flanked by two angels. He called me by my name and told me he came back to thank me for the wonderful burial tributes we gave him. He stretched his arms to shake my hands as I attempted to grab his hands, I woke up from the dream.

Jane told me how soothing my story was. She thanked me for the story, and suggested that I should include this story in my book. I was very happy that Jane was momentarily relieved of the grief and pain of her brother's loss during the taxi ride. Jane even smiled at me when she left my taxi, and I wished her well. This story serves as a tribute to my brother as well. I told Jane an abbreviated version of this story, however it contained all the highlights of the funeral. Despite the fact that this is a funeral account, this story would lift your spirits after you read it, and this is what African funerals entail.

Section IV
Driver/Passenger Relations

Chapter 48
Things Chicago Cabbies Dislike Most

Non Tipping Passengers

If you really want to ruin your taxi driver's day, you can do so easily by not giving him tip. As a cab driver, I know for a fact that every Chicago cabbie expect a tip at the end of the trip. This has become part of the taxi culture. Can you imagine how your waiter or waitress feels if you don't leave a tip for them? It is the same feeling that a cabbie has for non-tipping passengers. If you don't have extra money for tip, you will make them feel better by at least acknowledging the fact that they deserve a tip, than to just walk out without saying anything. They feel violated, and may run you down if you cross their path.

If you are giving them anything less than fifty cents, never tell them to keep the change. It is like adding salt to injury. A fifteen-percent tip is the norm, consider one dollar as the minimum tip for your cab driver. If you can give that much to Hotel doormen for taking your luggage inside, to the registration lobby, or for opening doors for you, it is a matter of fairness that you do the same to anyone you entrusted your life to, such as taxi drivers.

Don't Count Your Change Inside The Taxi

If you must pay them with change, don't start counting change as soon as you enter the taxi. Wait at least for the end of the trip. They don't carry a change box, and generally don't like being paid in coins, but coins are legal tender, so they are required to take them if it is your only option. I once had a passenger who counted change the entire trip and still was counting when I got to his destination. Eventually he paid me with a currency note, as I wondered what the point was.

Don't Tell Your Driver How Much Time You Have For The Trip

Chicago cab drivers are generally fast, and would take you to your destination in the shortest possible time. If your driver is a senior citizen, expect him to drive slower than younger drivers. Telling your cab driver to speed up or make this light would generally slow them down. They don't generally like commands, unless if accompanied with a promise for a greater tip, specified at the initiation of the trip.

Every passenger in Chicago usually runs late. Remember it is not the average ten-minute cab ride in the loop that will save you from being late. If you are late, it is not the taxi driver's fault, but yours. Next time leave earlier.

Passenger Tricks

Chicago cabbies know all the passenger tricks, so don't think you would outsmart them. Take for instance the case of a recent passenger I took to the Union Station. When I got to the corner of Monroe and Wacker, the fare was five dollars and ten cents, and traffic was very slow. My passenger decided to pay me off at that point, so he gave me six dollars, and requested a fifty-cent change leaving me with a forty-cent tip. He then sat back in the taxi and expected me to turn off the meter at that point.

I kept quiet and crawled with the traffic until I got to the Adams entrance to the Union station. The total fare on the meter was six dollars and thirty cents. He got up to leave the taxi; I informed him that he owed me a balance of eighty cents. He asked me why I did not turn the meter off when he paid me five dollars and fifty cents. I informed him that the taxi driver turns the meter off at the termination of the trip when the passenger disembarks from the cab. He paid me the balance of eighty cents. This story helps to illustrate the point here. Many loop passengers play this trick often; veteran drivers don't fall for that.

Don't Tell Them Stories About Taxi Rip Offs

Don't tell your cab driver about how your last driver ripped you off. Chicago cabbies generally don't do that. Cab drivers often are framed for taking longer routes. To avoid that, tell them your preferred way if you have one. More often than not, passengers choose longer routes as their preferred routes. I once picked up a New York tourist from the Wrigley field, going back to the Hyatt Regency on Wacker.

From my experience, New York tourists are generally more apprehensive than other passengers, for some reason. The other group that rivals New Yorkers in high apprehension level is Americans from small towns. I often refer to this syndrome as "small town mentality" But this New Yorker told me that the driver who brought him to the Wrigley field took a longer route.

He told me, not to take Lakeshore drive, because it was the longer way, the previous driver took. "Which way should I take?" I asked him. Take Clark all the way to the loop. I asked him how much he paid the previous driver. He said eleven dollars. I knew right then that this passenger was wrongly framing the other cabbie, because eleven dollars is the usual cost under normal traffic conditions, from the loop to Wrigley Ville.

So I took Clark at his request. The Cubs game just ended, and traffic around the Stadium is usually bad after Cub's games. We crawled along on Clark Street, and when we finally made it to the loop, the meter was twelve dollars and ninety cents. He did not say anything when he saw the fare, which was a simple vindication for the poor cabbie that brought him to the games. I did not want to make any remarks about the fare either. He paid me and walked away. I wonder which way he would take on his next trip to the Wrigley field.

If You Must Give Directions, Do It All The Way

If you must give your cabbie directions, do it all the way. Don't give them directions for part of the trip and expect them to figure out the rest of the route. They cannot read your mind. Don't blame them for the choice you made. If you don't want to choose a route, don't blame them for the route they chose. Chances are that they know better short cuts than you.

Chapter 49

Beating The Traffic In Chicago

Like other large cities, traffic congestion is a common problem in Chicago. Although Chicago is blessed with superior urban mass transit system, yet traffic on the city highways and streets would drive you crazy. The taxi driver has to carry out their business under such hectic conditions. This is no fun I can assure you. For me I have always sought alternative routes not only because my passengers are always in a hurry, but also it is a way to maximize my daily taxi income. The more runs I make, the more money I take home. Being tied up in traffic depresses the taxi driver's daily income. In this business, time is a critical factor.

Over the years, I have discovered alternative routes in and around the city. On a very bad traffic day in the city, a typical driving time from the loop to O'Hare airport could range from one hour to an hour and half, if you rely on the Kennedy expressway. A little known alternative route to O'Hare airport from the loop area is Elston Avenue. From the loop, take LaSalle to Division Street, and make a left turn on Division. Continue on Division to Elston Avenue. Make a right turn on Elston and follow Elston all the way to the end. Elston joins Milwaukee Avenue. Continue on Milwaukee Avenue to Devon Avenue. Make a left on Devon Avenue.

Continue on Devon to Higgins Avenue. Make a right on Higgins and go to Manheim Road. Make a left on Manheim Road, and O'Hare airport is ahead of you. This short cut would save you about thirty minutes of driving time to the airport on the days that the Kennedy expressway is really bad. You may do the reverse to the loop as well.

If you are going to the Midway airport during the evening rush hour, you may encounter a long delay along the I-55 South. Most traffic to the Midway airport uses the I-90/94 feeder ramp to I-55. Other Midway traffic from the loop uses south lakeshore to the I-55 ramp. This usually causes a long back up when lakeshore traffic merges with the I-90/94 feeder ramp. This causes a long delay on I-55 south up to Pulaski exit ramp. On a typical bad day, expect to spend about fifty minutes traveling from the loop to the Midway airport if you are using the I-55 expressway. But don't worry; there is an alternative route, which would cut your travel time in half. Simply head south on Clark Street from the loop.

Take Clark down to Archer Avenue in China Town. Take a right turn on Archer, and stay on Archer all the way to Cicero Avenue. Make a left turn on Cicero and the Midway exit ramp is two blocks ahead. This is a great little known Loop to Midway alternative route.

The Dan Ryan expressway is the major artery for traffic going to the Southside or to Indiana. During high traffic times, this could create a nightmare for commuters. But you don't have to languish on the Dan Ryan traffic, which literally crawls from the loop to 95th street. You may take south lakeshore drive to 57th street exit. Take 57th street to Stony Island Avenue. Continue south on Stony Island until you reach your cross street.

For those heading to Calumet City and Dolton, you may continue on Stony Island to the end, continuing on I-94 to Dolton and Sibley Boulevard exits. Harvey and Calumet Park traffic may also take Lakeshore south to Stony Avenue, and cut through 95th Street west to Halstead Avenue. Make a left turn on Halstead and head south.

Indiana traffic may also take lakeshore south to South shore. Continue south till you get to the Chicago Skyway entrance ramp {I-90 Toll road} to Gary and other Indiana points, including Gary/Chicago airports, and the Trump casinos.

Other Southside traffic may also use Halstead Avenue south as a great alternative route. These alternative routes would save you a lot of time particularly when the expressways are all clogged up.

Lakeshore drive is a great scenic drive along lake Michigan shores. Usually it is a fast way to Lincoln Park, North Broadway, Sheridan Road and Rogers Park. But if you are heading to the western areas of Lincoln Park, there are short cuts from the loop. You may take Orleans to Division, left to Sedgwick Avenue, make a right and go straight to North Avenue, or further North to Lincoln Avenue, a left turn on Lincoln Avenue would take you to the heart of Lincoln Park.

You may also take the lesser-known alternative routes to Lincoln Park. Take Grand Avenue from the loop to Kingsbury Avenue. Make a right on Kingsbury Avenue, to Chicago Avenue, make a left on Chicago Ave, and a right on Larabee Avenue. Take Larabee to Clybourn Avenue, and turn left on Clybourn. Take Clybourn to Ashland Avenue, and head North on Ashland until you reach your desired cross street. You may continue on Ashland to Rogers Park as well.

For those heading to Evanston from Chicago loop, take Lakeshore drive to Hollywood Avenue. It is always a good way to go. Continuing on Sheridan road as it winds around, it would eventually get you to the Northwestern University in the heart of the beautiful Evanston. Alternatively, from the loop, you may also jump onto the Kennedy and exit on Armitage Avenue. Make a right turn on Armitage Avenue to Ashland Avenue. Take a left on Ashland, and continue north until you get to Ridge Avenue. Make a left on Ridge and continue to Evanston.

Inside the loop, the lower Wacker drive system would really get you around only if you understand how to use it. Your best bet is the lower Wacker drive. You can travel underground on lower Wacker drive from Lakeshore drive to I-290 expressway, and vice versa. From Chicago financial district you may take the lower Wacker drive to Lower Michigan Avenue Bridge across Chicago River. Continue on Lower Michigan to Illinois street. Make a right on Illinois street and a left on Saint Clair. Another left turn on either Ontario or Huron streets would bring you to the heart of the magnificent mile. You may also continue straight on Illinois Street for the North Pier or the Navy Pier, or for access to both north and southbound lakeshore drive.

When heading up to the Gold Coast from the loop, most people normally would take Michigan Avenue, which is fine, but at times traffic on Michigan Avenue is so dense that an alternative route would get you there faster. You may take Dearborn Street or my favorite street-LaSalle street.

If you are coming into the loop from the Kennedy expressway, you may want to take alternative exit ramps if Ohio is backed up. The problem though is that there is no way to know if Ohio is clogged up or not until you get on it. My advice to you though is to avoid the Ohio ramp during the morning rush hour. If your destination is north of Chicago Avenue, your best bet is to take North Avenue, or Division exit ramps to LaSalle Street and make a right. If your destination is inside the loop, south of the Chicago River, you may try Washington, Monroe, or Jackson exit ramps.

Heading further south of Van Buren Streets and Lower Michigan Avenue, including Soldier field, take Congress Avenue exit, or Roosevelt exit, or I-55 east if you are going to the McCormick convention center.

Heading to the United Center from the loop for a major event could produce some unexpected delays. The reason being that basically United Center traffic from the loop usually takes Madison Avenue west. The United Center is located on Madison Avenue, near Damen intersection. You may beat the United Center traffic if you head west on Randolph Avenue, or Adams Street, leaving Madison Avenue to the tourists and Suburban traffic.

Often when large events end, traffic congestion is exacerbated for the simple reason that everyone leaves the stadium at the same time. Two ways you can beat the crowd is by leaving earlier than the crowd, or leaving later, allowing the traffic to clear up.

From the loop to the White Sox's Comisky Park you may avoid the massive congestion on Thirty-fifth Street, by taking the thirty-ninth street exit off the Dan Ryan expressway. This simple move may save you as much as fifteen to twenty minutes of traffic time.

Getting to the Cub's Wrigley field could be tricky. Again most traffic from the loop to the Wrigley field uses lakeshore to Belmont exit, creating a hefty back up on Belmont, Inner lakeshore drives, and Clark streets. An easier alternative would be lakeshore to Irving Park, west on Irving Park to Sheridan road. Take a left on Sheridan road, and the Wrigley field is about four blocks down the road. This alternative route may save you twenty minutes of traffic time. If you are coming to Wrigley field from the Northwest suburbs avoid Addison exit, which everybody else use. Take Irving Park road east to Clark Street, and turn right. Wrigley field is four blocks down on Clark and Addison Streets.

These alternative suggestions would really save you a lot of time sitting in the Windy city worsening traffic, but as bad as Chicago traffic may be, it is still better than that of New York or Los Angeles. I hope you'll find my short cuts helpful.

About the Author:

Paul Oranika is a Nigerian emigrant, a member of the Ibo tribe of Southeastern Nigeria. A Catholic by faith, he attended Morris Brown College in Atlanta, Georgia. He graduated with a B.A degree Cum Laude in Political Science, and was nominated to "Who is who among students in American Colleges and Universities" in 1981. He attended Clark Atlanta University where he obtained a Masters degree in Public Administration. Currently he writes news articles for London-based Offshore Investment Publication. Married with four children, Mr. Oranika is increasingly drawn to writing, and several magazines have published his articles.